First Look at...
Works 2.0 for the Mac

Keiko Pitter

Mitchell McGRAW-HILL

New York St. Louis San Francisco Auckland Bogotá Caracas Hamburg
Lisbon London Madrid Mexico Milan Montreal New Delhi Paris
San Juan São Paulo Singapore Sydney Tokyo Toronto Watsonville

Mitchell **McGRAW-HILL**
Watsonville, CA 95076

First Look at Works 2.0 for the Mac

1 2 3 4 5 6 7 8 9 0 DOH DOH 9 0 9 8 7 6 5 4 3 2

ISBN 0-07-050293-5

Sponsoring editor: Roger Howell
Editorial assistant: Laurie Boudreau
Director of production: Jane Somers
Production assistant: Leslie Austin
Project manager: Janelle Rohr, Bookman Productions
Interior designer: Renee Deprey
Cover designer: Janet Bollow
Cover photo: W. Warren/**West***light*
Compositor: Brent A. Jones
Printer and binder: R.R. Donnelley & Sons

Library of Congress Card Catalog No. 91-066890

Contents

Preface ix
Introduction xi

LESSON 1 **Microsoft Works: Common Features** **1**

Objectives 1
The Desktop 1
Mouse Commands and Menu Bar 2
Starting Up 3
Starting from a Hard Disk Drive • Starting from Two $3\frac{1}{2}$-inch Disk Drives • Open Dialog Box
Creating a New File 5
Saving a File 6
Using the Save As Command • Using the Save Command
Printing a File 8
Switching Between Files on the Desktop 9
Closing a File 10
Opening a File from Disk 10
Deleting a File 11
Works Help 12
Entering Commands from the Keyboard 13
Quitting Works 13
Summary 14
Self-Test 14

LESSON 2 **Word Processing: Creating Documents** **16**

Objectives 16
Starting Word Processing 16
Creating a Word-Processing File • Entering Text • Correcting Errors • Uppercase Letters
Saving Your Work 19
Deleting Text 19
Moving Text 20

Copying Text 21
Inserting or Replacing Text 21
Checking Spelling 22
Printing Text 23
Summary 24
Self-Test 25

LESSON 3 **Word Processing: Formatting Documents** **26**

Objectives 26
Retrieving a File 26
Formatting a Document 27
Page Setup 27
Margin Settings
Ruler Line 29
Line Indentation • Paragraph Indentation • Outdenting • Setting Tabs
Using Another File on the Desktop 33
Justification 34
Bold or Underline 35
Font or Size 36
Spacing 36
Copying Format 37
Summary 37
Self-Test 38

LESSON 4 **Word Processing: Editing Documents** **39**

Objectives 39
Cut and Paste 39
Entering Text Right Justified 40
Tab Alignment 42
Finding Text 43
Replacing Words 44
Paging 46
Page Numbering 47
Summary 47
Self-Test 48

LESSON 5 Spreadsheet: Creating a Simple Spreadsheet 50

Objectives 50
Creating a Spreadsheet File 50
Active Cell 51
Spreadsheet Size 52
Finding a Cell 52
Entering Data 53
Preparing the Worksheet 54
Entering Text 54
Correcting Errors
Entering Numbers 55
Entering Formulas 56
Saving Your Work 58
Printing the Spreadsheet 58
Summary 59
Self-Test 60

LESSON 6 Spreadsheet: Expanding and Formatting the Simple Spreadsheet 61

Objectives 61
Insert Command 61
Fill Right Command 62
Change Column Width 63
Sum Function 67
Saving a File Using a Different Filename 68
Printing the Spreadsheet with Horizontal Orientation 69
Summary 70
Self-Test 71

LESSON 7 Spreadsheet: Modifying the Display Format 72

Objectives 72
Change Display Format 72
Bold Characters • Justifying Text Entry • Display Format of Numbers

Cut or Copy and Paste 75
Deleting Columns 76
Formula Display 77
Moving Information Between Two Spreadsheets 78
Sorting Rows 78
Summary 80
Self-Test 81

LESSON 8 **Database: Creating Files** **83**

Objectives 83
Creating a Database File 83
Entering Field Names • Numeric Field • Entering Records
Saving Your Work 90
The List and Form Layouts 91
Changing the Field Display Width 92
Selecting and Printing a Record 92
Finding Information 93
Updating (Editing) the Record 94
Summary 94
Self-Test 95

LESSON 9 **Database: Manipulating the Data** **97**

Objectives 97
Arranging Records 98
Record Selection 99
Multiple Selection Rule 101
Numeric Range Selection 102
Changing Field Display Order 103
Inserting a Record 104
Copy Records 105
Deleting a Record 106
Quick Save 107
Summary 107
Self-Test 108

LESSON 10 **Database: Printing a Report and Changing Structure** 109

Objectives 109
Defining a Report 109
Saving a Report 114
A Report Containing Selected Records 114
A Report Containing Selected Fields 115
Displaying Total 117
Changing Database Structure 118
Insert a Field • Delete a Field
Summary 119
Self-Test 120

LESSON 11 **Moving Information Between Applications** 121

Objectives 121
Moving Information from Spreadsheet to Word Processor 121
Moving Information from Spreadsheet to Database 124
Moving Information from Database to Spreadsheet 125
Moving Information from Database to Word Processor 125
Merging Information in the Database into a Word-Processing Document 127
Summary 130
Self-Test 131

Self-Test Answers 132

Works 2.0 for the Mac Command Summary 134

Works 2.0 for the Mac Keyboard Commands 140

Index 141

Preface

First Look at Works 2.0 for the Mac is a step-by-step, hands-on tutorial covering the fundamentals of Microsoft Works on the Mac. You can use this book as a self-paced guide, in a lecture class, or as a supplemental text in a variety of classes.

First Look at Works 2.0 for the Mac will quickly get you "up to speed" with the program's most useful features. Complete with a comprehensive command summary at the end of the book, *First Look at Works 2.0 for the Mac* makes reference quick and easy.

ORGANIZATION

Each lesson contains the following features:

- A list of objectives discussed in the lesson
- A hands-on tutorial that guides you through specific functions and commands
- A chapter command summary that includes the page number where each command was first introduced
- A self-test that reinforces learning

As you work through *First Look at Works 2.0 for the Mac,* you will create files that are used in later lessons. For this reason, it is suggested that you use your own data disk for file storage and retrieval. This book assumes that you already have some familiarity with the Macintosh interface.

FIRST LOOK AT... SERIES

This book is part of the First Look at... series, which consists of titles designed to cover the most popular commercial software packages.

The purpose of each book in this series is to provide an inexpensive, quick, and complete learning tool that you can use for ready reference after you've completed the tutorial. At the end of each book, a comprehensive summary of commands makes reference easy. It is assumed that you have access to the complete software package and all its features.

In a minimum number of pages, each book covers the most commonly used features of a particular program—enough to equip students with fundamental proficiency in a short time.

ACKNOWLEDGMENTS

I extend much gratitude to the staff of Mitchell/McGraw-Hill, especially Roger Howell and Laurie Boudreau, for much patience and understanding. Wendy Brashares, Evergreen College, and Fred Hanzelin, South Suburban College, gave me helpful suggestions.

I changed jobs in the midst of this project, but found strong support for my writing at my new place of employment, Willamette University. My newly acquired lab assistants, Tom Butler, Seth Danielson, and John Sulek, painstakingly went over the manuscript. I also received much encouragement and support from Vice President Todd Hutton of Willamette University. To all, thank you very much.

As always, I send special thanks to my children Greg and Jackie for their love and understanding.

Keiko Pitter
Salem, Oregon

Introduction

Three of the most popular uses of computers today are word processing, electronic spreadsheet, and database management.

- A **word processor** lets you apply the power of computers to the creation and handling of texts such as letters, memos, contracts, and reports. The text is stored in the computer, allowing you to easily edit and format it. The text can then be stored on disk and printed by a printer attached to the computer.
- An **electronic spreadsheet** provides capabilities for generating and formatting worksheets (multicolumn accounting reports) in computer memory, and for entering and manipulating data within worksheets. It is used much like a pencil, a sheet of paper, and a calculator. It can be a useful tool when repetitive calculations or recalculations are needed.
- A **database management system** is a software tool for building and manipulating a collection of data. It is a computerized filing system that allows you to store information and quickly retrieve any of this information in whatever format and medium you wish.

Ordinarily, you have to buy several separate software packages to be able to perform all of these tasks, or applications. However, there are problems associated with the use of more than one software package. For one thing, different software packages use different commands to accomplish the same thing. (Although with Macintosh there is a somewhat standardized set of instructions. For example, ⌘-C is the Copy command in almost all Macintosh software.)

The second problem is data integration. Results required by users often extend beyond one application area. A businessperson who is writing a report may need spreadsheet figures, or a clerk ordering supplies may want information from the inventory database. The problem in using separate software packages is that information created by one program cannot always be shared electronically with another program. To use the result produced by one program in another, you may have to reenter the information. Furthermore, although it is possible to run multiple applications simultaneously on a computer, most people still do not own such a system. Often, the computer can only run one program at a time and you cannot easily switch back and forth between applications.

These problems have led to the creation of **integrated software packages**, which combine several applications. Because it is one software package, the commands used in different applications are similar. Also, you can switch from one application to another, and information created by one application can easily be used in another.

Microsoft Works is an integrated software package that combines word-processing, spreadsheet, database management, and communications. In the next eleven chapters, you will get a quick introduction to the use of the Microsoft Works word processor, spreadsheet, and database management system. (Communications is not covered in this book.) There are many options and features available in Microsoft Works. You can explore these on your own after you understand the basic commands.

LESSON ONE

Microsoft Works: Common Features

OBJECTIVES

In this lesson you will learn how to:

- Recognize the concept of desktop.
- Use mouse and keyboard terminology.
- Start Microsoft Works.
- Create a new file.
- Save a file.
- Print a file.
- Close a file.
- Open an existing file.
- Delete a file.
- Use the Help information.
- Quit Works.

THE DESKTOP

Computerized processing of information in Microsoft Works is similar to processing information by hand. Suppose that you are a clerk in a business office and are preparing bills for customers. Suppose also that you are working without a computer—that is, you are processing these bills by hand. You pull out information on all the customers. Better yet, you select information on only those customers who owe you money. You also get out your company's policy on late payment penalties. You need your calculator, pencil, typewriter, and some blank sheets of paper. You look at a customer record, do some calculations, type a late notice, record information on the customer record, and so on. You are working with information on your desk and using a typewriter and calculator.

This is precisely how Microsoft Works processes information. The documents you prepare using the word processor, the spreadsheet you create, and the information you store in a database, all go on the **desktop,** which is the random access memory (RAM) of the computer. Moreover, each document, spreadsheet, and database is known as a **file**.

Just as your desk is not a permanent storage area, neither is the Works desktop. Those files left on the desktop are lost when you turn off the computer. If a file is important, you must store a copy in a more permanent storage place, such as a disk. You can have up to 14 different files on the desktop at the same time, although you can work with only one at a time. The number depends on how much memory your Macintosh has and how large your files are. If you want to remove some of these files to display new ones, you can. Putting a file on the desktop is called **opening a file,** and removing a file from the desktop is called **closing a file.**

MOUSE COMMANDS AND MENU BAR

Although this book assumes that you are familiar with the basic operation of the Macintosh, we will review a few terminologies and operational procedures.

Menu Bar	A menu that appears along the top of the screen.
Pull-down Menu	A menu that appears as a result of pointing and holding down the button on an option, such as from the Menu Bar. When making a selection from the pull-down menu, do not release the button. Simply move (drag) the pointer to a selection so that it is highlighted and then release the button.
Title Bar	A bar at the top of a window that indicates the name of the file or application that is displayed in the window.
Window	A viewing area of a portion of computer memory as displayed on the screen.
Close Box	A little square box at the top left corner of each window. When you click on the close box, that window closes.
Scroll Bar	Bars at the right edge and bottom of a window that allow you to view those portions of the screen not currently visible in the window. Click on the arrow keys at either end of the Scroll Bar to move the content of the screen.
Icon and Label	Graphic symbol and name of an application.
Mouse Pointer	Single-headed arrow controlled by moving the mouse.
I-beam	A type of pointer shaped like the capital letter "I" and used for entering and editing text.

Point	Place the arrow on top of an object, such as an icon or a button.
Click	Press the mouse button once.
Double-click	Press the mouse button twice in rapid succession without moving the mouse.
Drag	After positioning the mouse pointer on an object, press and hold down the mouse button while moving the mouse. When the new position is reached, release the button.
Select	Point and click on an object. When making a selection from the Menu Bar, however, you do not release the mouse.

STARTING UP

In this lesson, you will be introduced to the basic commands common to all applications in Microsoft Works. You will have a chance to briefly practice each of these commands. Those commands that have more involved options, such as printing, will be explained in detail later.

The commands covered here are the ones you will need each time you use Works. Try to familiarize yourself with them. If you forget, you can refer back to this section.

To work with software on a computer, the computer must be turned on and the software launched.

Starting from a Hard Disk Drive

Step A. Turn on your Macintosh.

Step B. Double-click the hard disk icon. That is, point to the hard disk icon using the mouse and click the mouse button twice.

Step C. If there is a folder for Microsoft Works, double-click on it.

Step D. Double-click the Microsoft Works icon. The Microsoft Works icon is shown in Figure 1-1.

Figure 1-1

Starting from Two 3½-inch Disk Drives

Step A. Turn on your Macintosh.

Step B. Insert the Works Startup disk into one drive.

Step C. Insert the Works Program disk into the other drive.

Step D. Double-click the Works Program disk icon. That is, point to the Works Program disk icon using the mouse and click on the mouse button twice.

Step E. Double-click the Microsoft Works icon. The Microsoft Works icon is shown in Figure 1-1.

You will now try this on the computer:

Using one of the above two methods, start Works.

Works displays the **Open dialog box** as shown in Figure 1-2.

Figure 1-2

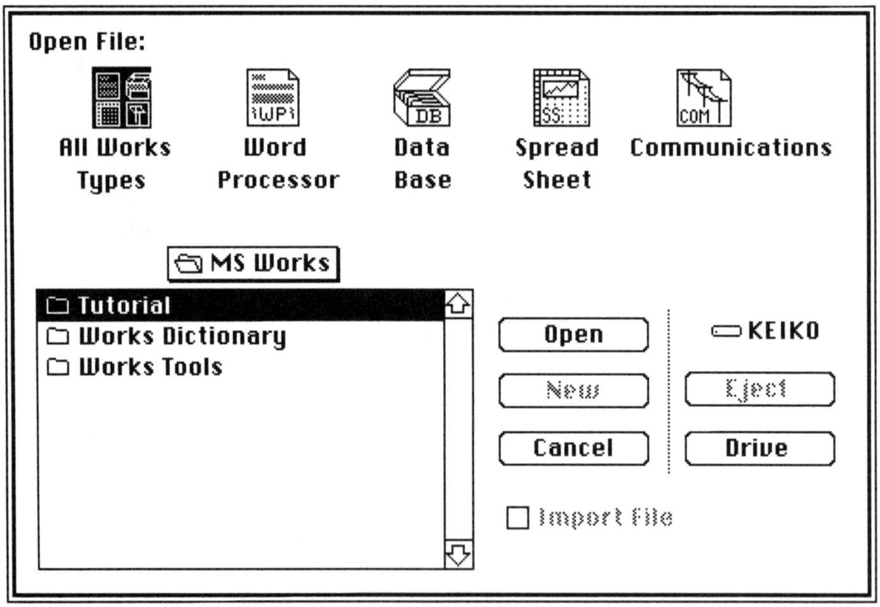

Open Dialog Box

The Open dialog box is the starting point for various applications and features available in Works. You can create new files from this dialog box, as well as open existing files on a disk.

Along the top of the dialog box are **application icons.** They show types of files you can choose from. The first icon, All Works Types, is already selected.

It is the **default** selection, which means the computer assumes that to be your selection unless otherwise specified.

On the bottom right are various buttons. To activate a button, you point and click the mouse. When a button name is dimmed, that option is not available to you at that time. On the bottom left is the **list box,** which shows a list of all files and folders in the **current disk or folder.** The current disk or folder is the one that the computer uses to save or retrieve files.

The name of the current folder or disk is displayed just above the list box. Also, the name of the current disk is displayed above the Eject button on the right. The current disk or folder can be changed.

If you need to change the current folder, click and hold down the mouse button on the folder name above the list box. A pull-down menu appears displaying the name of the current disk and/or other folders on the current disk. Drag the mouse pointer to the disk or folder name you want and release the mouse button.

If you need to change the current disk, click on the Drive button. If the Drive button is dim, the option is not available to you. That is, there are no other drives. The current disk name changes each time you click the Drive button. When the name of the disk you want is displayed, stop.

If you need to eject a disk (so that you can change disks), click the Eject button. If the Eject button is dim, your current disk is not a floppy disk and cannot be ejected.

CREATING A NEW FILE

You can create a new file in Works from either the Open dialog box or from the New command.

To create a new file from the New command,

Step A. Choose **New** from the **File** menu. That is, point at the **File** option on the Menu Bar. Press and hold down the mouse button. A pull-down menu appears. Drag the pointer down to the **New** command (so that it is highlighted).

Works displays the Create New Document dialog box.

Step B. Click the icon for the application tool you want to use.

Step C. Click the **OK** button.

To create a new file from the Open dialog box,

Step A. Click the icon for the application tool you want to use.

Step B. Click the **New** button.

You will notice that the New button is dimmed right now. This is because you have not specified the application tool you plan to use.

Use one of the above methods and open a word-processing file.

A blank word-processing file appears. You will note that the file name that appears on the Title Bar is Untitled (WP).

Untitled is the default filename for any new file. (WP) is displayed to show that you are using the word-processing application tool. (SS) is displayed for a spreadsheet file and (DB) for a database file. When you save the file, you will give it a more descriptive name.

To make this a legitimate word-processing file, you will enter some text.

Type your name and press Return.

SAVING A FILE

The file on the desktop is sitting in the RAM (temporary memory) of the computer. If you turn off the computer or if there is a power failure, you lose that file. That is why it is important that you save the file on a disk, not only when you quit Works, but frequently during your Works session. Once a file is on a disk, it is permanently stored. Should there be a power failure, you can retrieve the most recent version of the file from the disk and continue with your work.

NOTE: As mentioned in the preface, you will save all your files on your own data disk.

Insert your data disk in the floppy drive. If you are working with two floppy drives, you should replace the Works Program disk with the data disk. You will be asked to reinsert the program disk later.

If your data disk has not been formatted (prepared to store data), the computer will prompt you to do so.

When you save a file, you have two choices: you can use the **Save** command or the **Save As** command.

- If you use the Save command, the file is saved using the filename that appears on the Title Bar. If there already is a file by that name on the disk, the new file will replace the other file.
- If you use the Save As command, you type a new name for your file.

As mentioned earlier, when you create a new file, Works automatically gives it a default name, Untitled, and this is the name that appears on the

Title Bar. When you save the file for the first time, you use the Save As command and give it a more meaningful name. A filename can include any characters except colons, including spaces and both uppercase and lowercase letters.

Using the Save As Command

Step A. Choose **Save As** from the **File** menu.

The Save As dialog box, similar to the one shown in Figure 1-3, is displayed.

Figure 1-3

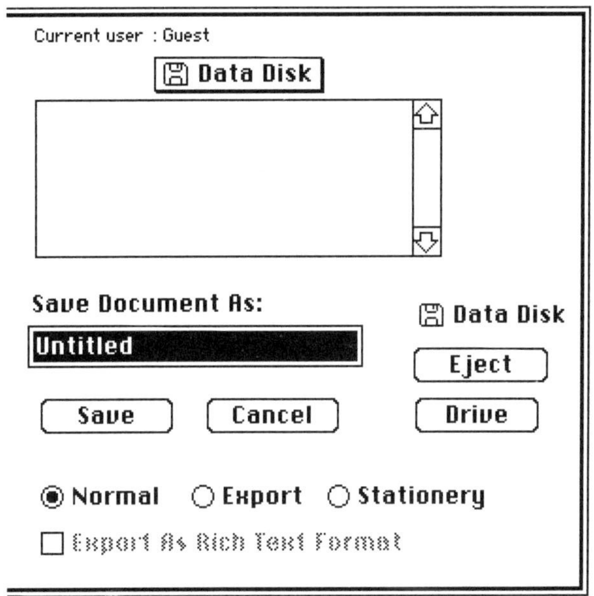

Step B. Type a name for the file.

The new name you type replaces the one in the text box.

Step C. Make sure to select the appropriate drive to save the file. Use the **Eject** button if you need to change to another disk.

Step D. Click the **Save** button.

If there already is a file with that name on the disk, Works asks you if you want to replace it. You can replace it, or cancel the command.

The file is saved, and you can continue using the file.

Using the Save Command

Step A. Choose **Save** from the **File** menu.

The file is saved, and you can continue working.

NOTE: The first time the file is saved using the Save command, the Save As box appears so that you can enter a filename other than Untitled.

Now you will save the current file using a different name.

1. Choose **Save As** from the **File** menu.

   The Save As dialog box is displayed. You see the filename Untitled.

2. Type the filename **MY NAME**.

   The new filename replaces the old filename.

3. Change the current drive, if needed.

4. Click the **Save** button.

   The file is saved, and you return to the document. The Title Bar now displays MY NAME.

PRINTING A FILE

When printing the content of a file, you will adjust the format of the output, depending on which application tool you are using. Printing will be covered in detail in appropriate chapters. In general, to print a file, you choose Print from the File menu, set options, and click the OK button. Right now, you will print the document that is currently on the desktop. Options available to you through the Print dialog box will depend on the printer you are using. This manual shows the dialog boxes for both an ImageWriter and a LaserWriter printer.

NOTE: It is usually a good idea to save the file before printing. This way, should anything go wrong, you can start over by retrieving the file from the disk.

1. Make sure that the printer is on and is ready to use.

2. Choose **Print** from the **File** menu.

   The Print dialog box similar to the ones shown in Figures 1-4(a) and 1-4(b) appears.

3. You can leave most options on the default settings. If you need to change any, click on the appropriate buttons.

Figure 1-4(a)

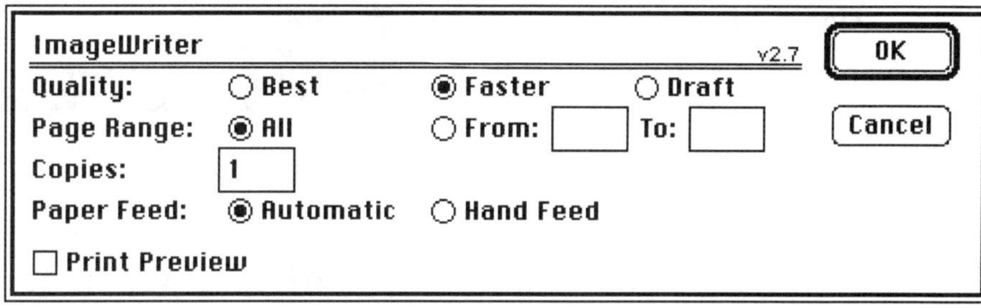

Figure 1-4(b)

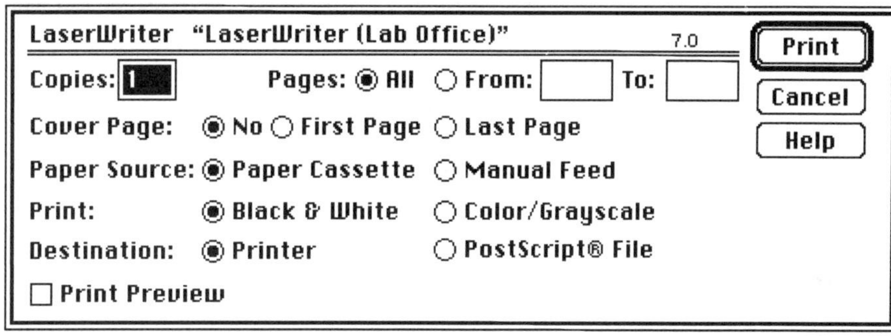

4. When options are set, click the **OK** or **Print** button to start printing.

   Your file is printed.

Should you want to cancel the printing for some reason, hold down the Command key (⌘) and type a period.

SWITCHING BETWEEN FILES ON THE DESKTOP

It is possible to have more than one file open on the desktop at the same time.

1. Open a second word-processing file by choosing **New** from the **File** menu.

   A new document named Untitled appears on the screen.

You have two files on the desktop: one is called MY NAME and the other one is Untitled. Files on the desktop appear as choices on the Window menu. To go from one file to another, all you need to do is to choose the file you want to use from the Window menu.

2. Display the **Window** menu.

   You see filenames MY NAME and Untitled as menu options as shown in Figure 1-5.

Figure 1-5

3. Choose MY NAME from the **Window** menu.

   The file MY NAME is now displayed.

CLOSING A FILE

When you want to remove a document from the desktop, you close it.

Step A. Choose **Close** from the **File** menu, or click the close box in the upper-left corner of the window.

Step B. If you've made changes to the document since you last saved it, Works asks if you want to save the changes. You need to respond accordingly.

Let's close the file MY NAME.

Choose **Close** from the **File** menu.

The file Untitled is now displayed.

Although the file MY NAME is removed from the desktop, it still exists on the disk. You can always retrieve the file from the disk and work on it some more.

OPENING A FILE FROM DISK

Retrieving a file onto a desktop is also known as opening a file. To open a file, choose Open from the File menu. The Open dialog box is displayed. To open an existing file on a disk, select the name of the file from the list box and click the Open button. When the All Works Types icon is highlighted, all Works files on the disk are listed. If you want to narrow your choice, then you can click on one of the four application icons. If you click on the Word Processor application icon, for example, only word-processing files on the disk are listed in the list box.

1. Choose **Open** from the **File** menu.

   The Open dialog box is displayed.

2. Select the file MY NAME from the list box and click on the **Open** button.

   The content of MY NAME is displayed.

3. Close the file MY NAME.

DELETING A FILE

Deleting a file means to remove it from the disk. This is different from removing it from the desktop. When you remove a file from the desktop, if you had previously saved it on the disk, you can retrieve it from the disk. When you delete a file from the disk, however, it is gone permanently. A file is deleted from a disk only if you know that you will never need this file on this disk (and are sure of it).

You will now delete the file MY NAME from the disk.

NOTE: You cannot delete a file from the disk unless there is another file open on the desktop.

1. Choose **Delete** from the **File** menu.

   The Delete dialog box, as shown in Figure 1-6, is displayed. The list box shows all files on the current disk or folder.

Figure 1-6

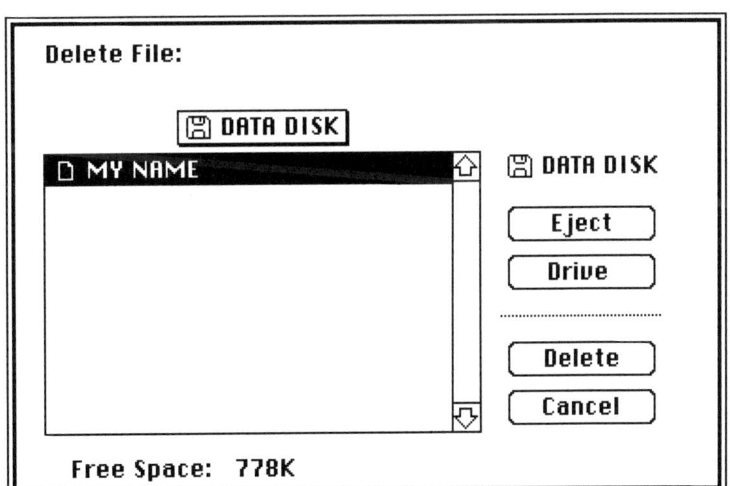

2. Select the file MY NAME.
3. Click the **Delete** button.

   Works asks you to confirm that you want to delete the file.
4. Click the **OK** button to delete it.

   The file is deleted from the disk.

WORKS HELP

Microsoft Works has a **Help screen** that gives a brief explanation of all commands on the Menu Bar and refers you to a page number in the Microsoft Works manual.

To get help on a command,

Step A. Choose **Help** from the **Window** menu.

The Help window appears as shown in Figure 1-7.

Figure 1-7

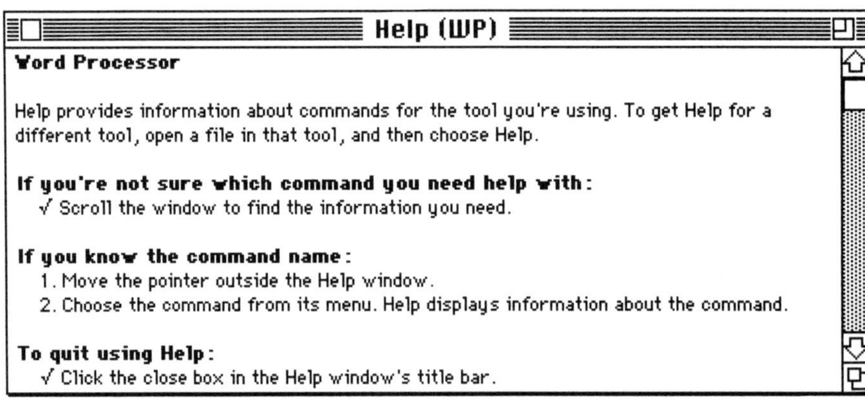

NOTE: During the Help mode, the pointer turns into a question mark when it is outside the Help window.

Step B. Choose the command you want help on just as you would normally choose a command from the Menu Bar.

Step C. To close the Help window, click its close box.

NOTE: You cannot access the Help command unless there is a file open on the desktop.

You will now look at Help for the Open command.

1. Choose **Help** from the **Window** menu.
2. With the question mark cursor, choose **Open** from the **File** menu.

   The Help window changes to display information on the Open command.
3. Click on the close box to exit the Help mode.

ENTERING COMMANDS FROM THE KEYBOARD

As various pull-down menus were displayed, you may have noticed that after certain command options Works displays Command key (⌘) options. For example, after the Quit command in the File menu, it displays ⌘-Q. You can invoke many menu options from the keyboard by holding down ⌘ and pressing a key. To use the Save command, for example, rather than using the mouse to select the File menu and drag to click on the Save command, you can hold down ⌘ and press S.

This book does not discuss these keyboard options as various commands are introduced. Pull-down menus display equivalent keyboard options when available. The list of keyboard commands is included in the Command Summary at the end of the book.

QUITTING WORKS

At the end of each Works session, do the following:

1. Choose **Quit** from the **File** menu.
2. For each file you worked with (created new or made changes in) but did not save, an alert box will appear asking if you want to save the changes. Respond accordingly.

   You exit Works.
3. Choose **Shut Down** from the **Special** menu.
4. Turn the computer off, if needed.

■ SUMMARY

Topic or Feature	*Command or Reference*	*Menu*	*Page*
Launch Microsoft Works	Double-click on MS Works icon		3
Create a New File	New	File	5
	Click on the application tool icon, then click the New button		5
Save a File with New Name	Save As	File	6
Save a File with the Same Name	Save	File	6
Print a File	Print	File	8
Switch Between Files	Filename	Window	9
Close a File	Close	File	10
Open a File	Open	File	10
Delete a File	Delete	File	11
Help	Help	Window	12
Quit Microsoft Works	Quit	File	13

■ SELF-TEST

1. You can have up to ________ file(s) open on the desktop at the same time.
2. When you select an object with a mouse, you point and ______________.
3. To make a selection on the pull-down menu, you ______________________ ____.
4. To start Microsoft Works, you ____________ on the Microsoft Works icon.
5. The ______________ option is the selection that the computer assumes unless otherwise specified.
6. To change the current disk, you click on the __________________ button.
7. The Works program assigns the filename ______________________ as the default filename for any new file.

8. The ______________ command lets you save a file with a new filename.
9. The close box is a square located on the ______________ corner of the window.
10. When you delete a file, the file is erased from the ______________.

LESSON TWO

Word Processing: Creating Documents

OBJECTIVES

In this lesson you will learn how to:

- Use word-processing terminology.
- Create a word-processing file.
- Enter text in an empty word-processing file.
- Save a file on a disk.
- Scroll the text.
- Delete a block of text.
- Move or copy a block of text.
- Insert or replace text in an existing document.
- Check spelling.
- Print the text.

STARTING WORD PROCESSING

First, start your computer and launch the Works program. Follow the instructions given in Lesson One so that the Open dialog box is displayed.

Creating a Word-Processing File

To enter text, you must first create a word-processing file.

1. Click on the Word Processor application icon.
2. Click on the **New** button.

   An empty word-processing window is now displayed, as shown in Figure 2-1 on the following page.

In the middle of the Title Bar, the document name appears, along with (WP) to show the part of Works you are currently using.

Figure 2-1

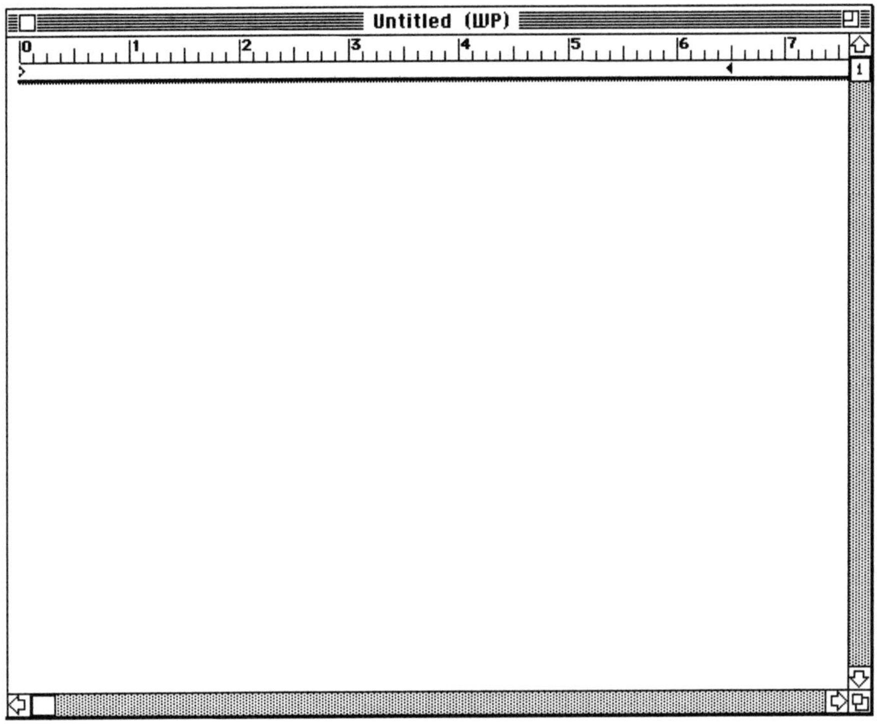

Under the Title Bar is the **Ruler Line**. The Ruler Line shows you the relative distance from the left margin. It also displays the document margin settings relative to the left margin (indent markers). In a new document, tab stops are preset at every half inch on the ruler, but you can't see them. These will be discussed in the next lesson.

At the top left corner of the screen is a blinking vertical bar, called the **insertion bar**. The insertion bar shows the position on the screen where your entries are made. Works always inserts letters at the insertion bar.

NOTE: To position the insertion bar in a text, place the I-beam where you want the insertion bar to be and click the mouse.

Entering Text

To enter text, use your keyboard just like a typewriter. As you enter a character, it appears at the insertion bar position, and the insertion bar moves to the right one position. However, unlike the keyboard on a typewriter, this keyboard needs no carriage return as you fill up a line on the screen. Just keep on typing, because when the insertion bar gets beyond the right margin, it will reappear at the left margin, one line down. When you come to the end of a paragraph, [Return] must be pressed. [Return] breaks the line and moves the insertion bar to the leftmost position, one line down. You have to press [Return] once at the end of a paragraph or twice if you want to insert a blank line between paragraphs in the text.

If your text fills up the screen, the text will **scroll up**— a new line will appear at the bottom of the screen, and the uppermost line will disappear.

Correcting Errors

If you make a typing error, you can delete unwanted characters by pressing [Delete]. You can then retype the text.

NOTE: On some Macintosh keyboards, [Delete] *is labeled* [Backspace].

Uppercase Letters

To type uppercase letters, hold down [Shift] while you type the character, just as you would on a typewriter. If you want to type a series of uppercase characters, press [Caps Lock] so that it is in the down position. To return to lowercase, press [Caps Lock] again so that it is in the up position. When you enter special characters such as $ and), you need to hold [Shift] down regardless of the [Caps Lock] position.

PRACTICE TIME

Enter the following text:

> **Records of transactions, contracts, and inventories form the basis that allows business to be conducted in an orderly manner. Scribes have been used through the ages to produce copies of business contracts. Inventions which have lowered the cost or increased the speed for an individual to write a document have resulted in increased business productivity. These inventions include paper, ball point pens, and typewriter. The personal computer did not become a success until it became useful for business. Today, word processing is the most common business use of personal computers.**

As you typed this paragraph, you might have noticed the phenomenon called **word wrap**. This means that as the text gets to the right margin, a word that is too long to fit on the line is moved intact to the next line. Words are not split between two lines.

Had this been a long document where the entire text could not be displayed on one screen, you could display any part of the document by using the vertical Scroll Bar.

NOTE: You can scroll the screen by clicking on the up and down arrow keys on the vertical Scroll Bar.

SAVING YOUR WORK

You must save your text on a disk if you plan to use it during another session. Lesson One describes how you save files on disk. You will use the filename My File to save to your data disk.

1. Choose **Save As** from the **File** menu.

   The Save As dialog box appears, with the original name Untitled selected.

2. Type **My File**.

   My File replaced Untitled.

3. Make sure that the correct drive is selected.

4. Click the **Save** button.

   Works saves the document as a new file on the disk, and changes the name on the Title Bar.

   You return to the document.

DELETING TEXT

As you recall, if you make a mistake when you are typing text, you can correct it immediately by

Step A. Pressing [Delete] to remove unwanted characters.

Step B. Typing the correct text.

You may delete unwanted characters anywhere in the text by

Step A. Placing the insertion bar to the immediate right of the characters you wish to delete.

Step B. Pressing [Delete] to erase unwanted characters.

Step C. Typing the correct text.

Delete removes the character to the left of the cursor. If you want to delete 100 characters, you have to press Delete 100 times. There is an easier way to delete a block of the text.

1. Place the I-beam to the left of the first character of the second sentence. That is, to the left of the character "S" of "Scribes have...."
2. Hold down the mouse button and drag until you've highlighted the text "Scribes have been used through the ages to produce copies of business contracts," then release the button. (See Figure 2-2.)

Figure 2-2

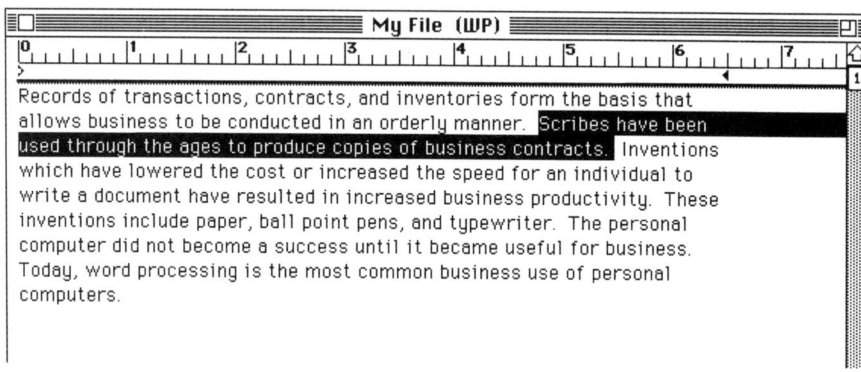

NOTE: If you highlighted the wrong section of text by mistake, simply reselect the text.

3. Press Delete.

   The highlighted text disappears.

MOVING TEXT

If you want to move a section of text, such as a sentence, from one location to another, you do the following:

1. Place the I-beam immediately after the next to the last sentence—on the blank space following the word "business."
2. Hold down the mouse button and drag until you've highlighted the sentence "Today word processing is the most common business use of personal computers."
3. Choose **Cut** from the **Edit** menu.

   The quotation disappears. It's stored on the Macintosh Clipboard.

The **Clipboard** holds information temporarily in your computer's memory until you cut or copy another selection.

4. Position the I-beam on the space just before the fourth sentence—after the word "typewriter"—and click the mouse so that the insertion bar is positioned there.

5. Choose **Paste** from the **Edit** menu.

   The text from the Clipboard is placed at the insertion bar position.

COPYING TEXT

It is also possible to copy a block of text. Copying text is different from moving text in that the highlighted text is not deleted from the original position. Select Copy from the Edit menu, instead of Cut.

INSERTING OR REPLACING TEXT

If you need to insert a word in the middle of a sentence or a sentence in the middle of a paragraph, position the insertion bar where you want to insert the text and start typing. Any text to the right of the insertion bar will be pushed across the line and down the page of your screen to make room for your insertion.

1. Place the insertion bar before the word "Inventions" in the second sentence.

2. Type the following text just as it appears (*with errors*):

   The earliest writing, cuneiform inscriptoins on on clay tablets, often kept business recrds.

   The text will now look like Figure 2-3 on the following page.

When making changes in text, you don't always just insert characters. More often, you replace the current words with other words. You can delete the previous entry and then insert, but you can also replace characters. All you need to do is highlight the characters you want replaced and type the characters you want.

1. Highlight the words "personal computers" in the last sentence.

2. Type **microcomputers**.

   The text is replaced.

Figure 2-3

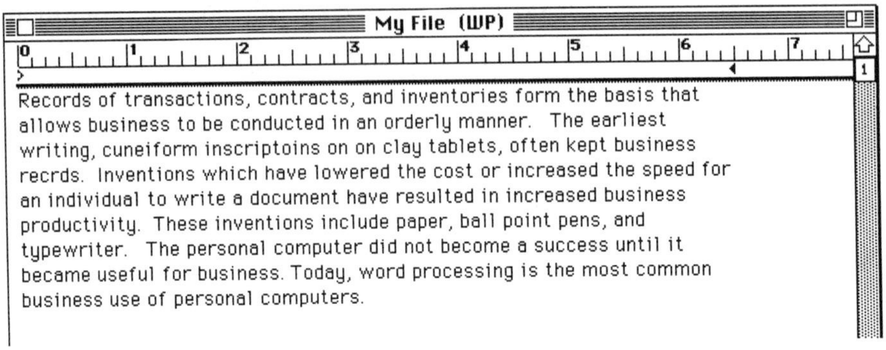

CHECKING SPELLING

You entered a sentence with errors in the current document. You will now correct these errors by checking the spelling. When you enter commands to check spelling, Works compares each word in the document with a list of correctly spelled words, known as the **dictionary**. The program flags those words that are not in the dictionary, and, for each of these words, it displays words from the dictionary that you might have meant.

1. Choose **Correct Spelling** from the **Spell** menu.
2. If necessary, locate the Works Dictionary folder; be sure that the dictionary file, MsWorksDict, is selected in the list box, and click the **Open** button.

NOTE: To open the dictionary, you may need to change disk drives, disks, and/or folders. If necessary: click the folder name above the list box to change folders; click the Drive button to change disk drives; and click the Eject button to change disks. Once you've located the dictionary, Works will remember its location the next time you check spelling.

The minute you locate and open the Works dictionary file, the computer begins to scan the document for spelling errors.

Works highlights the word "inscriptoins" and suggests that you replace it with "inscriptions" as shown in Figure 2-4 on the following page.

3. Click the **Replace** button to correct the error.

   Works questions "on on," and suggests that you replace it with "on."

4. Click the **Replace** button to correct the duplicate word.

   Works now finds the misspelled word "recrds," but it recommends "recreant" as the replacement.

Figure 2-4

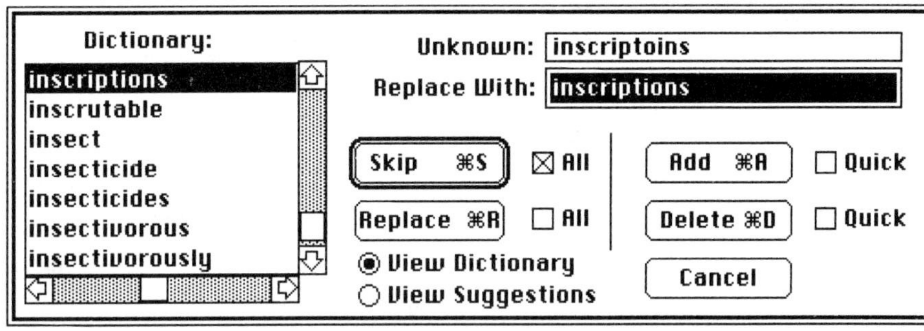

5. Scroll the list box on the left upward until "records" comes into view. Click the word, and then click the **Replace** button.

NOTE: Many words are not in this dictionary. If the word is not included in the dictionary, you can type in your own spelling in the Replace With: box and select Replace.

When the spelling correction is complete, Works displays the number of words scanned and number of errors found. Follow the instructions on the screen to continue.

6. Click on the **OK** button.
7. Select **Save** from the **File** menu.

   The current document replaces the one on the disk.

PRINTING TEXT

You will now print the text.

1. Make sure that your printer is turned on and is ready to use.
2. Choose **Print** from the **File** menu.

   The Print dialog box similar to the ones shown in Figures 2-5(a) and 2-5(b) is displayed.

Figure 2-5(a)

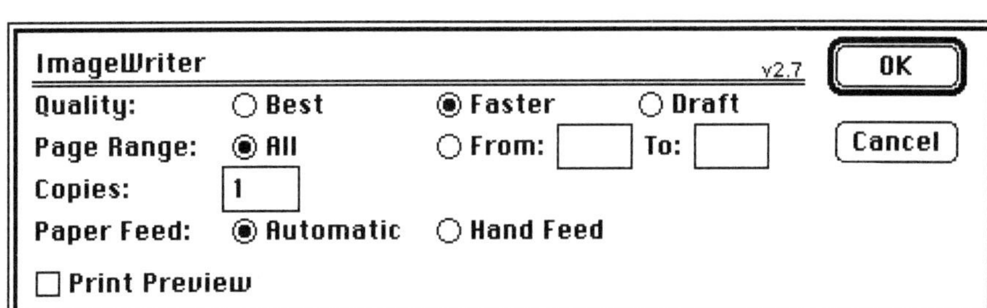

Figure 2-5(b)

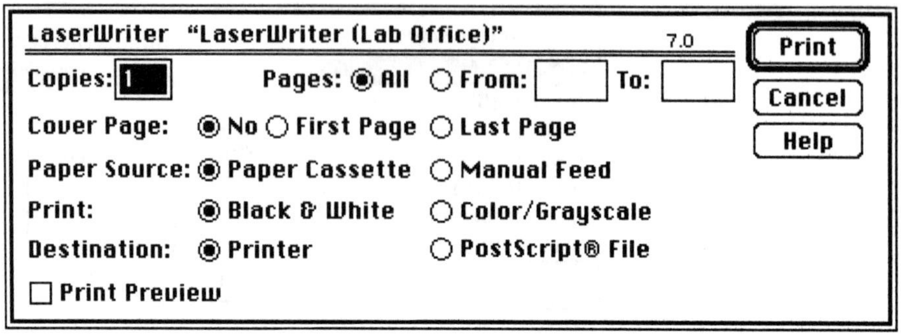

3. Change the options, if needed.
4. Click the **OK** or **Print** button.

   Your document is printed.

This is the end of this lesson. Quit Works as described in Lesson One.

■ SUMMARY

Topic or Feature	*Command or Reference*	*Menu*	*Page*
Delete Text	Place insertion bar to the right of error and press Delete		18, 19
Select (Highlight) Text	Position the I-beam at the beginning of the text to be highlighted and drag the mouse		20
Move Text	Select text, then Cut; position the insertion bar where you want text moved, then Paste	Edit Edit	20
Copy Text	Select text, then Copy; position the insertion bar where you want text moved, then Paste	Edit Edit	21
Insert Text	Place the insertion bar where you want text inserted, then type text		21
Replace Text	Select text to be replaced, then type new text		21

Topic or Feature	*Command or Reference*	*Menu*	*Page*
Check Spelling	Correct Spelling	Spell	22
Print File	Print	File	23

■ SELF-TEST

1. When the pointer is positioned within the document, it turns into a(n) ______________________________.
2. During text entry, you press Return at the end of a ______________ and when you want to insert a ______________.
3. When you position the I-beam on the text and click on the mouse, it turns into a(n) ______________________________.
4. A section of text can be selected (highlighted) by ______________________________ ______________________________ ______________________________.
5. When you Cut or Copy text, it is placed on a ______________.
6. The difference between Cut and Copy is that when you ______________ a text, it is removed from the document; whereas when you ______________, it stays intact in the original document.
7. Text on the Clipboard can be inserted in a document by selecting the ______________ command from the Edit menu.
8. If you highlight a section of text, then type new text, the new text ______________ the highlighted text.
9. A document can be printed by selecting the Print command from the ______________ menu.
10. The spelling checker ______________ (can/cannot) detect all spelling errors.

LESSON THREE

Word Processing: Formatting Documents

OBJECTIVES

In this lesson you will learn how to:

- Retrieve a file.
- Recognize some of the default format settings.
- Specify page setup.
- Set format on the Ruler Line for:
  left and right indentation
  first line indentation
  paragraph indentation
  outdenting
  tab stops
- Use the Format menu for:
  justification
  bold or underline
  spacing
- Copy format.

RETRIEVING A FILE

Start your Macintosh and launch the Works program so that the Open dialog box is displayed. Make sure that your data disk from Lesson Two is in the drive.

First you will retrieve the text from the last lesson. Do you remember how to load it?

1. Click on the Word Processor application icon.
2. Make sure that the drive for your data disk has been selected.
3. Highlight My File and click on the **Open** button.

   The text from the previous lesson is displayed on the screen.

FORMATTING A DOCUMENT

When you printed the text at the end of the last lesson, you might have noticed that it was printed similar to the way it was displayed on the screen. Since the screen display format you used was preset by Works (you were using the default settings), the document may not have been printed in the format you wanted.

You can change the way your document is formatted. There are three places where the appearance of a document is specified: the Page Setup dialog box, the Ruler Line, and the Format menu.

- The Page Setup dialog box is where you indicate the paper size, margin settings, and printing orientation. These specifications affect the entire document.
- The Ruler Line is where you specify indentation of text relative to the margin settings, the width of text on the page, and the tab settings. The settings on the Ruler Line affect a paragraph. When you set an option on the Ruler Line, it affects the paragraph the insertion bar is currently in. You can change the format of any paragraph by positioning the insertion bar anywhere in the paragraph and specifying the new setting. You can change the format of multiple paragraphs by highlighting them with the mouse and specifying the format desired.
- The Format menu lets you specify such formatting options as justification, size, style (underline, bold), appearance (font), and spacing of text. When you set options in the Format menu, some of the settings affect the paragraph that the insertion bar is in, and others affect the text until another setting is specified. You can also change the appearance of text already entered by highlighting it and specifying the format desired.

PAGE SETUP

First you will specify formatting through the Page Setup command.

Choose **Page Setup** from the **File** menu.

The Page Setup dialog box, similar to those shown in Figures 3-1(a) and 3-1(b), is displayed.

NOTE: The Page Setup dialog box is different, depending on the printer you are using.

The Page Setup command lets you specify paper size, printing orientation, special effects, headers, footers, and margins. These settings affect the

Figure 3-1(a)

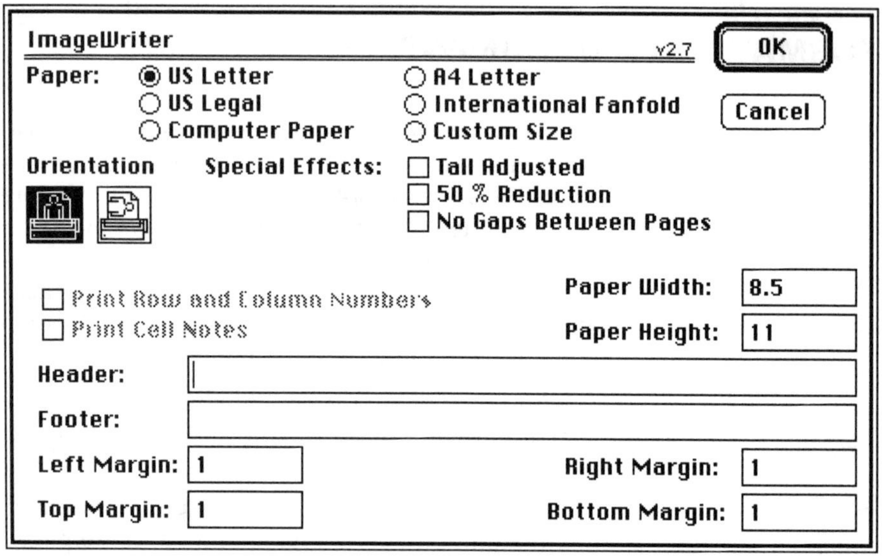

Figure 3-1(b)

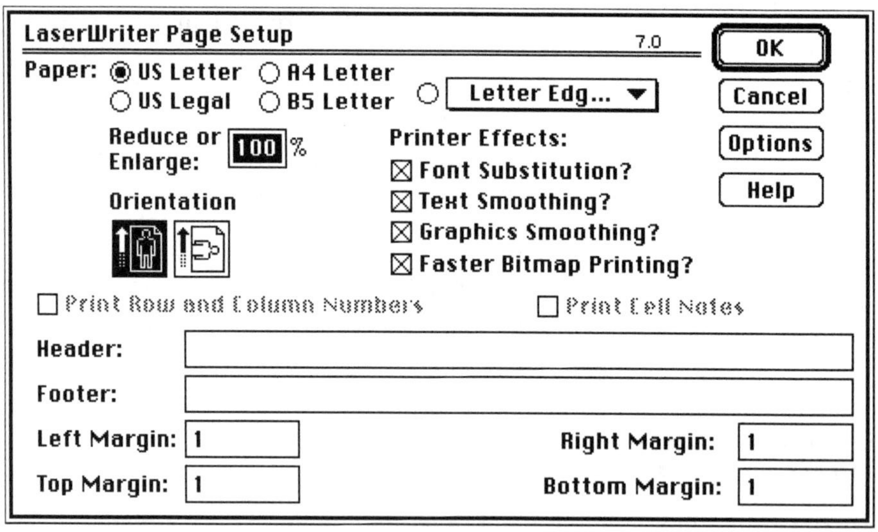

appearance of the entire document. To change the settings, click on the appropriate options. Notice that by default the paper selected is a standard (U.S. letter) 8½" by 11".

Margin Settings

As you can see, the default setting for all margins is 1 inch. You will now change the left margin to 2 inches.

1. Press [Tab] until the left margin box is highlighted.
2. Type **2**.
3. Click the **OK** button.

   You will get the warning box as shown in Figure 3-2.

Figure 3-2

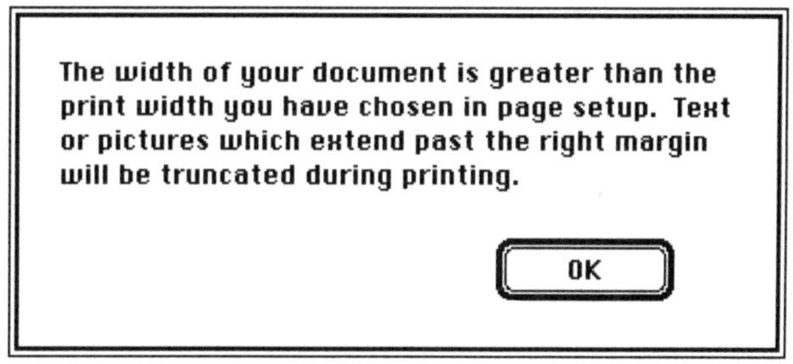

   Initially, the document My File was written 6½ inches wide to accommodate an 8½" by 11" paper with both left and right margins set to 1 inch. When you increased the left margin to 2 inches, the 6½-inch-wide text no longer fit on the paper. Hence, you need to change the text width to 5½ inches. You specify this on the Ruler Line.

4. Click the **OK** button for now.

   You return to the document.

5. If the ruler is not showing, choose **Show Ruler** from the **Format** menu.

RULER LINE

At the top of the document, you see a Ruler Line. (See Figure 3-3.) The first line indent marker ■ and the left indent marker ▸ are both positioned at 0 inches. The right indent marker ◂ is positioned at 6½ inches. The left indent marker tells how much the text is to be indented relative to the left margin. The right indent marker tells the line width. The first line indent marker is explained later.

In this case, you need to move the right indent marker to the 5½-inch position to accommodate the new left margin setting.

   Drag the right indent marker along the ruler to the 5½-inch position.

   The text adjusts accordingly.

Figure 3-3

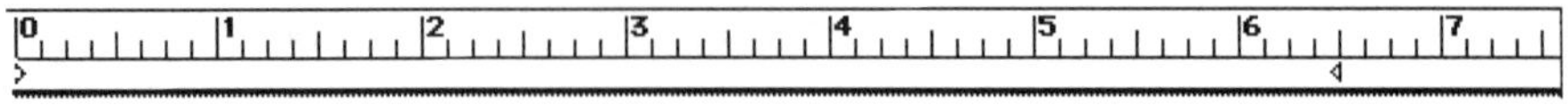

PRACTICE TIME

1. Change the right margin setting to 2 inches.
2. Change the Ruler Line setting accordingly.
3. Print the text.

Now add a new word-processing file to the desktop.

NOTE: Any changes in Page Setup for My File are internal to My File. The new file you just added still carries all the default settings.

Line Indentation

Suppose you want to indent the first line of a paragraph by ½ inch. You will accomplish this by moving the first line indent marker to the ½-inch position on the Ruler Line. The first line indent marker ■ is at the same position as the left indent marker ▸. Once the first line indent marker is positioned, you just type the text and Works automatically indents the first line of the paragraph for you. All you need to do is press Return at the end of each paragraph.

1. Make sure that the Ruler Line is showing.
2. Carefully drag the first line indent marker to the ½-inch position. If you drag the left indent marker by mistake, move the first line indent marker then place the left indent marker back at the 0-inch position as shown in Figure 3-4.

Figure 3-4

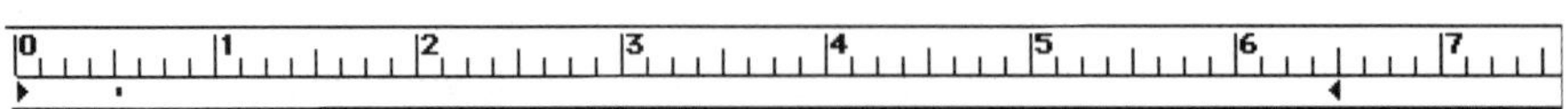

PRACTICE TIME

1. Enter the following text:

   When a computer is instructed to do a job, it handles the task in a very special way. It accepts the information. It stores the information until the information is ready to be used. It processes the information. Then it gives out the processed information.

2. Print the text.
3. Save this file on your data disk as FILE 2.

Paragraph Indentation

Sometimes, you need to indent a whole paragraph for emphasis, such as when you are quoting from a book. To do this, change the values of the left and right margins for the paragraph.

To indent an entire paragraph, place both the left indent marker and the first line indent marker in the same position.

1. Place the insertion bar at the end of the text.
2. Insert at least one blank line.
3. Drag the left indent marker to the same position as the first line marker.
4. Type the following:

   The concept behind word processing is a fascinating one. The typewriter has become archaic, stricken by a single technological blow. The concepts of training and productivity have changed, too. The more productive worker is the one who can insert text changes, make corrections, move blocks of text, and otherwise process text rewrites efficiently.

5. Press Return to insert a blank line.
6. Move the left indent marker to the 0-inch position, so that the text is indented only on the first line.
7. Type the following:

   We no longer train people to type 60-plus words per minute, error free.

8. Save the text using the **Save** command.
9. Print the text.

Outdenting

You can also outdent a paragraph, known as a **hanging paragraph**. In contrast to indenting the first line of a paragraph, outdenting a paragraph means the first line of the paragraph extends to the left.

1. Delete the second and third paragraphs.

2. Make sure that the cursor is positioned two lines below the end of the text.
3. Enter the following:

   When a computer is instructed to do a job, it handles the task in a very special way.
4. Press [Return] twice.
5. Move the left indent marker to the 1½-inch position.
6. Move the first line indent marker to the 1-inch position.
7. Move the right indent marker to the 5½-inch position.
8. Enter the following. Be sure to press [Tab] after each number.

   1. It accepts the information.

   2. It stores the information until it is ready to be used.

   3. It processes the information.

   4. It gives out the processed information.

   Your screen should look as displayed in Figure 3-5.
9. Save the file as FILE 3.

Setting Tabs

Tabs are set by default every ½ inch, but you cannot see them on the Ruler Line. You can remove these by setting your own tabs. When you set a tab, all default settings to the left of the new ones are erased.

- To **set a tab**, you position the pointer in the blank area below the ruler marking where you want to set the tab, and then click the mouse. There

Figure 3-5

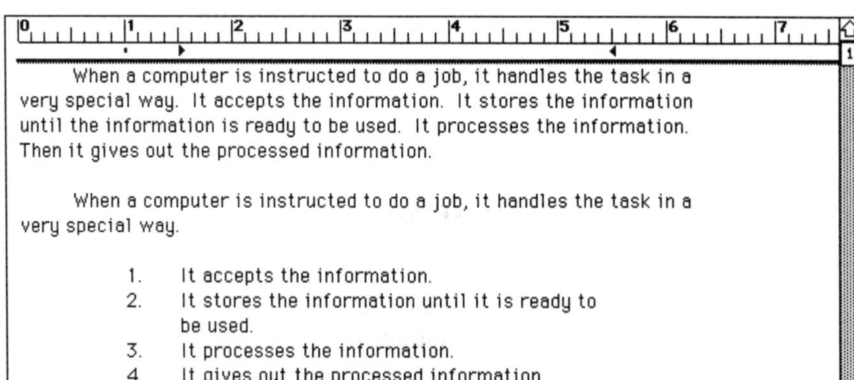
When a computer is instructed to do a job, it handles the task in a very special way. It accepts the information. It stores the information until the information is ready to be used. It processes the information. Then it gives out the processed information.

When a computer is instructed to do a job, it handles the task in a very special way.

1. It accepts the information.
2. It stores the information until it is ready to be used.
3. It processes the information.
4. It gives out the processed information.

are four types of tab alignments: left, right, decimal, and center. One click generates a left tab, two a right tab, three a decimal tab, and four a center tab. Right and decimal tabs are discussed in the next lesson. The effect of using center tab is not discussed.

- To **move a tab**, just drag it to a new location.
- To **remove a tab**, drag the tab down into the text. When you release the button, the tab disappears.

Right now, let's set a left tab at the 1¼-inch position.

1. Make sure that the Ruler Line is displayed.
2. Move the I-beam to the left of the sentence "1. It accepts ..." and select the next four sentences.
3. Point to the 1¼-inch position in the Ruler Line.
4. Click the mouse.

   The left tab stop appears and text shifts to reflect the new tab set, as shown in Figure 3-6.
5. Move the left indent marker to the same position as the tab at the 1¼-inch position.
6. Save the file as FILE 4.

USING ANOTHER FILE ON THE DESKTOP

You will now use the file My File on the desktop.

Figure 3-6

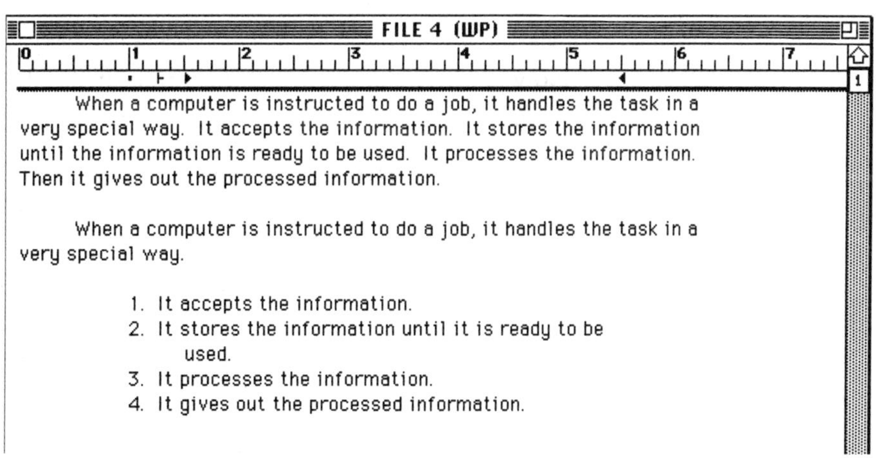

Select My File from the **Window** menu.

The text for FILE 4 disappears, and the text for My File appears.

JUSTIFICATION

The default setting for text justification is Left. That means that the left margin is aligned, but not the right margin. The alignment of text can be changed through the Justification option in the Format menu.

1. Choose **Justification** from the **Format** menu. *Do not release the mouse button.*

   A list box appears to the side as shown in Figure 3-7. The check mark in front of Left indicates that the left justification has been selected. If you select Justified, both the left and right margins will be aligned.

2. Release the mouse button.

Figure 3-7

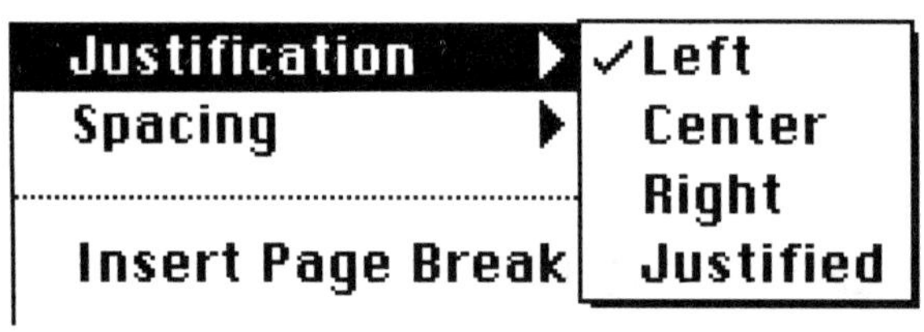

When you specify the justification, it affects the paragraph that contains the insertion bar. You can also change the justification of multiple paragraphs by selecting them with the mouse and specifying the justification.

Now you will change the alignment to Justified.

1. Position the insertion bar anywhere in the paragraph.

2. Choose **Justification** from the **Format** menu, but do not release the mouse button. Drag the mouse to select the **Justified** option in the list box.

   The text on the screen adjusts as shown in Figure 3-8.

If you want to center text, such as when you enter a title, you position the insertion bar where you will enter the text, specify Center justification, and start typing.

1. Position the insertion bar at the beginning of the text.

Figure 3-8

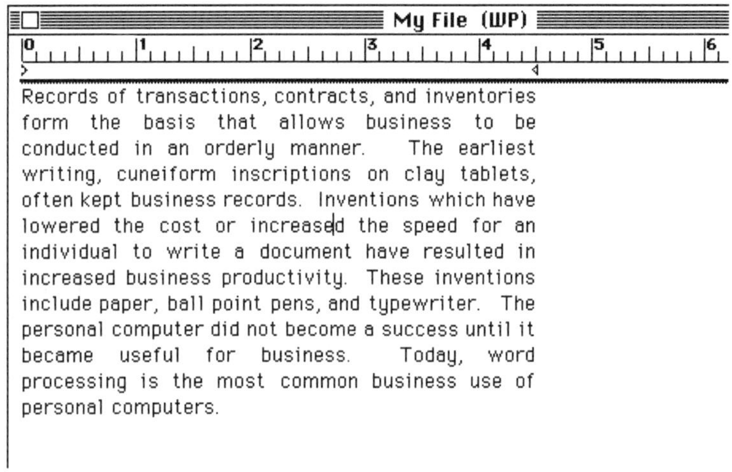

2. Press [Return] twice to insert two blank lines.
3. Position the insertion bar on the first line.
4. Specify **Center** justification.
5. Type **WORD-PROCESSING EXAMPLE.**

   As you type, the characters appear in the middle of the line, centered between the line indent markers.

BOLD OR UNDERLINE

Suppose that you want the title to appear in bold characters. You can probably figure out how to do this.

1. Select the title with the mouse.
2. Choose **Style** from the **Format** menu. Drag the mouse to select **Bold** in the list box.

   The title is now in bold characters.

3. Position the insertion bar at the end of the text, then press [Return] to insert a blank line.

If you want characters to appear in boldface as you type, you can enter the specification for bold. Then the characters that follow will be in bold until you enter a specification to stop it.

1. Choose **Style** from the **Format** menu, then specify **Bold**.

You could not see it, but a check mark appeared in front of Bold.

2. Type the following:

   This text is entered as bold characters.

3. To turn off the bold style, choose **Style** from the **Format** menu, then specify **Bold** again.

   This removes the check mark that was in front of the Bold option.

4. Now type the following: **The characters are no longer in bold.**

NOTE: To turn the bold style on and off more easily, you can enter ⌘-B. *That is, hold down* ⌘ *and press the character* ***B****.*

Underlining text works the same as bold. You can choose Underline from the Format-Style menu, or enter ⌘-U. You can experiment on your own with the other styles on the menu. They all work the same way.

FONT OR SIZE

Font refers to the design used to print characters, and size is just that—the size of the characters. In general, the larger the size number, the larger the print.

Changing the font or size of the characters works the same way as bold and underline. You select (highlight) the text to be affected, then choose Font or Size from the Format menu and drag to select the appropriate selections. You can also make the appropriate selection from Font or Size in the Format menu, then type the text. The types of fonts or number of sizes available depends on your particular setup.

SPACING

Microsoft Works lets you specify single, one and one-half, and double spacing. The spacing is set from the Format menu. Spacing affects the paragraph that contains the insertion bar. You can also change the spacing of multiple paragraphs by selecting them with the mouse and choosing the appropriate spacing.

1. Position the insertion bar anywhere in the first paragraph.
2. Choose **Spacing** from the **Format** menu. *Do not let go of the mouse.*

   A list box appears with several options.

3. Drag the mouse to select **Double**.

   The first paragraph is now double-spaced.

PRACTICE TIME

1. Change back to single spacing.
2. Switch to FILE 4.
3. Change the format of the first paragraph of FILE 4 to Justified, one and one-half spacing.

COPYING FORMAT

Once you have specified the format for a paragraph, you can copy the format to another paragraph. Right now, you will copy the format of the first paragraph to the second. The format includes indentation.

1. Position the insertion bar anywhere in the first paragraph.
2. Choose **Copy Format** from the **Format** menu.
3. Position the insertion bar anywhere in the second paragraph.
4. Choose **Paste Format** from the **Format** menu.

   The format of the second paragraph is the same as the first.

This is the end of this lesson. Quit Works as described in Lesson One. There is no need to save any of the files.

■ *SUMMARY*

Topic or Feature	*Command or Reference*	*Menu*	*Page*
Specify Paper Size, Printing Orientation, Headers, Footers, and Margins	Page Setup	File	27
Show Ruler Line	Show Ruler	Format	29
Set Text Width, Indentation of Text Relative to Left Margin, and Tab Settings	Ruler Line		29

Topic or Feature	*Command or Reference*	*Menu*	*Page*
Set Justification	Justification	Format	34
Bold Text	Choose Bold from Style	Format	35
Underline Text	Choose Underline from Style	Format	35
Select Font	Font	Format	36
Select Size	Size	Format	36
Set Spacing	Spacing	Format	36
Copy Format	Copy Format	Format	37

■ SELF-TEST

1. Margins can be changed from the __________________ dialog box.
2. The ____________ marker tells how much the text is to be indented relative to the left margin.
3. When you set margins to a value greater than the default value, you must change the text width on the _____________________________.
4. The first line indent marker tells how much to indent the __________ of the paragraph.
5. Tabs can be set by ____.
6. You can remove a tab by __________________________________.
7. When the justification is set to Justified, ____________ (left/right/both) margin(s) is(are) aligned.
8. You can switch to another document on the desktop from the ____________ menu.
9. You can change the display style of selected text by choosing the ________ command from the ___________ menu.
10. To copy the format of a paragraph to another paragraph, you position the insertion bar ______________ (at the beginning of/anywhere in) the paragraph and choose __________ from the Format menu.

LESSON FOUR

Word Processing: Editing Documents

OBJECTIVES

In this lesson you will learn how to:

- Cut and paste a block of text from one word-processing file to another.
- Enter text with right or decimal justification.
- Find a particular word or combination of words in a text.
- Replace a particular word or combination of words in a text with a specified word or combination of words.
- Understand the concept of paging.
- Print page numbers.

Your Macintosh should be started and the Works program launched so that the Open dialog box is displayed. Make sure that you have the data disk from Lesson Three and that the proper drive for the data disk has been selected.

You will start by retrieving My File and FILE 2 from the data disk.

PRACTICE TIME

Open files My File and FILE 2.

CUT AND PASTE

Sometimes you need to take a passage out of one document and include it in another. In Microsoft Works, information from one document can be cut onto a Clipboard. That information can then be pasted into other word-processing documents.

In placing information on the Clipboard, the information can be copied (the original stays intact) or cut (the original is deleted).

1. Display FILE 2 on the screen.

   You will copy the second paragraph from FILE 2 into My File.

2. Select the second paragraph with the mouse.
3. Choose **Copy** from the **Edit** menu.

   It looks as though nothing happened, but a copy of the highlighted text has been placed on the Clipboard. Let's look at the Clipboard.

4. Choose **Show Clipboard** from the **Window** menu.

   The content of the Clipboard is displayed as shown in Figure 4-1.

Figure 4-1

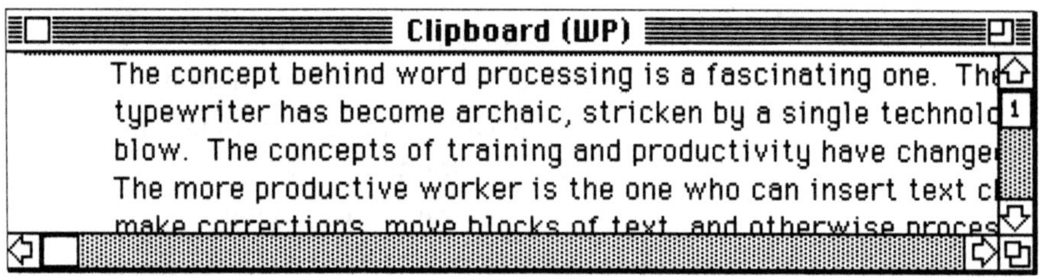

   The content of the Clipboard will remain there until other information replaces it. Only one piece of information can be on the Clipboard at a time.

5. Choose **Hide Clipboard** from the **Window** menu.
6. Switch to My File through the **Window** menu.
7. Place the insertion bar at the end of the document.
8. Press [Return] a couple of times to insert a blank line.
9. Choose **Paste** from the **Edit** menu.

   The paragraph from FILE 2 is now part of My File as shown in Figure 4-2 on the following page.

ENTERING TEXT RIGHT JUSTIFIED

Usually, you want your text aligned at the left. If you want the text to be aligned at the right as well, you set justification to Justified. There are times, however, when you want the text to be entered right justified (aligned at the right margin) without regard to the left margin. An example might be when you are entering the date at the beginning of a letter.

Figure 4-2

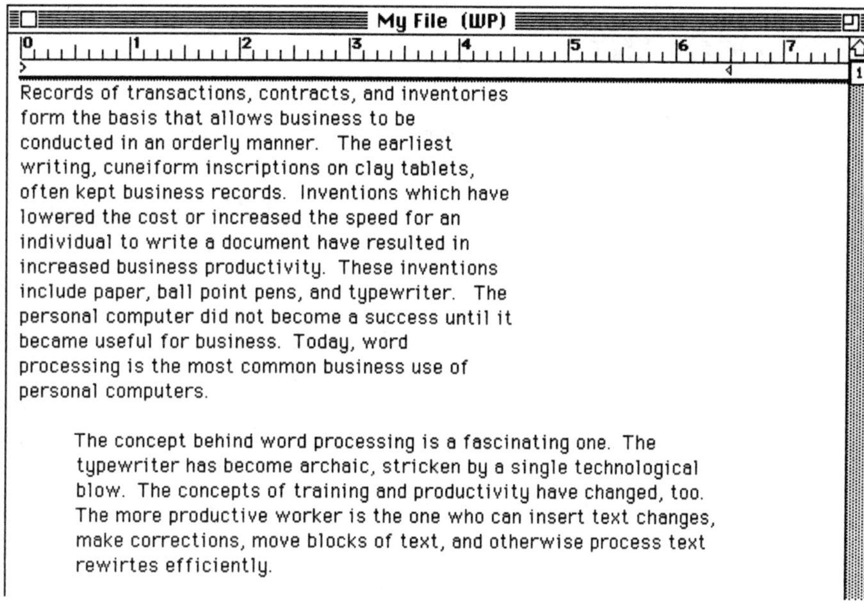
My File (WP)

Records of transactions, contracts, and inventories form the basis that allows business to be conducted in an orderly manner. The earliest writing, cuneiform inscriptions on clay tablets, often kept business records. Inventions which have lowered the cost or increased the speed for an individual to write a document have resulted in increased business productivity. These inventions include paper, ball point pens, and typewriter. The personal computer did not become a success until it became useful for business. Today, word processing is the most common business use of personal computers.

The concept behind word processing is a fascinating one. The typewriter has become archaic, stricken by a single technological blow. The concepts of training and productivity have changed, too. The more productive worker is the one who can insert text changes, make corrections, move blocks of text, and otherwise process text rewirtes efficiently.

1. Open a new word-processing file.
2. Set **Justification** to **Right**.

   The insertion bar appears at the position of the right indent marker.
3. Type **December 14, 1992** and press [Return].

   The text is entered right justified—even with the right margin.

PRACTICE TIME

1. Enter the partial letter given below. You can work around the date that is already entered.

   1728 Forest Road
   Takoma Park, Maryland
   December 14, 1992

   Mr. Gary Bradshaw
   Computer Parts Shop
   1234 Byte Street
   Golden, Colorado 81234

   Dear Mr. Bradshaw:

   Please process my order for the following items:

2. Save the text as LETTER 1.

TAB ALIGNMENT

In the letter you started, the next step is to specify the items you want to order, quantity, and price, as shown below:

50	high density disks @14.75	$737.50
5	printer ribbons @11.95	59.75
1	diskette container @9.95	9.95

You will enter the first column right justified at 1 inch; the second column is entered left justified at 2 inches; and the third column is entered aligned at the decimal point at 5 inches. You can set the tabs so that this type of data entry is simple. (See Lesson Three for how to set and delete tabs.)

You will set tabs at 1 inch, 2 inches, and 5 inches. However, you want a right tab at 1 inch; a left tab at 2 inches; and a decimal tab at 5 inches.

1. Make sure that the insertion bar is at the bottom of the letter in the LETTER 1 file. There should be at least one blank line after the end of the text.
2. Position the pointer at 1 inch and click *twice* for a right tab.
3. Position the pointer at 2 inches and click *once* for a left tab.
4. Position the pointer at 5 inches and click *three* times for a decimal tab.

   The Ruler Line should be as shown in Figure 4-3.

Figure 4-3

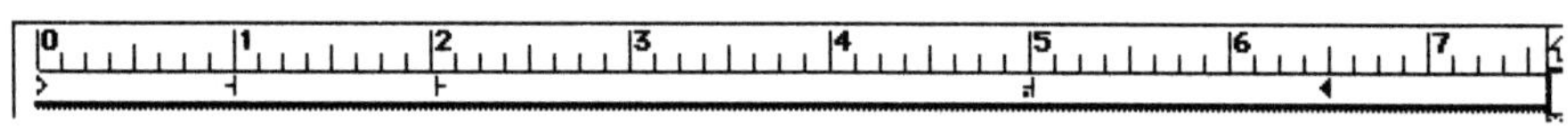

5. Press [Tab].

   The insertion bar jumps to the 1-inch position.
6. Type **50**.

   The entry is right justified at the 1-inch position.
7. Press [Tab].

   The insertion bar jumps to the 2-inch position.
8. Type **high density disks @14.75**.

   The entry is left justified at the 2-inch position.
9. Press [Tab].

   The insertion bar jumps to the 5-inch position.

10. Type **$737.50**.

    The entry is made with the decimal point at the 5-inch position.

11. Press [Return].

PRACTICE TIME

1. Type in the next two items.
2. Insert a blank line after the third item.
3. Delete all current tab settings.
4. Set a left tab at the 3½-inch position.
5. Enter the rest of the letter. (The closing appears at the 3½-inch position.)

   My check for $807.20 is enclosed.

   Yours very truly,

   (your name)

   Enclosure

6. Save the letter again with the same file name.

FINDING TEXT

There are times when you need to find a specific word that you know is somewhere in the document. Microsoft Works has a command to help you do just that.

1. Switch to My File.

You need to find the word "cuneiform" because you have additional information you want to insert.

2. Choose **Find** from the **Search** menu.

   The Find dialog box appears as shown in Figure 4-4.

Works is asking what text you want to find. It will find all occurrences of the text (characters), disregarding uppercase or lowercase. The text may even be embedded in another word. That is, if you search for "and," Works will

Figure 4-4

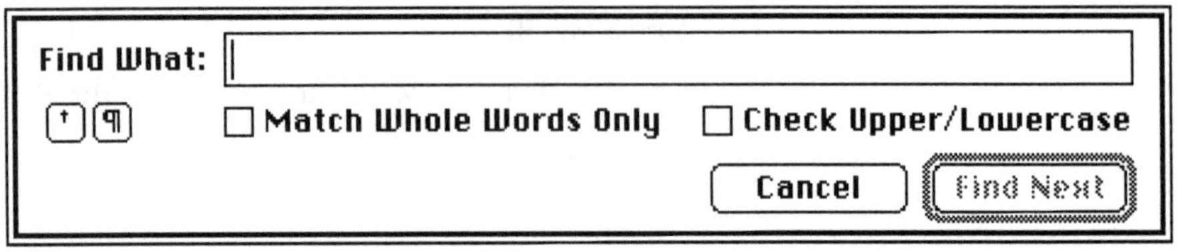

find "hand," "band," or any other word that has "and" embedded in it. If you want Works to ignore such occurrences, click on the first option, "Match Whole Words Only." If you want Works to pay attention to uppercase and lowercase occurrences of the text, click on the second option.

3. Type **cuneiform**.
4. Click the **Find Next** button.

   The word "cuneiform" is highlighted.

   If you want to find the next occurrence of the same text, click the **Find Next** button again. When there are no more occurrences of the text, you will get a dialog box informing you of such.

PRACTICE TIME

Find all occurrences of the word "productivity" in My File.

*NOTE: When you choose Find from the Search menu, "cuneiform" still appears as the search text. Just type **productivity**. It will replace the previous entry.*

REPLACING WORDS

When editing a document, sometimes you are looking for a particular word that needs to be replaced. For example, suppose you had written a rather lengthy report on a client only to find out that there has been a change in the client's company name. Rather than searching through the entire document visually, looking for the occurrences of the company name and replacing the name, you'd like Works to find and replace them for you.

PRACTICE TIME

1. Start a new word-processing document.
2. Enter the following text, then save it as LETTER 2.

(today's date)

Mr. Smith
Personnel Office
Republic Engineering
3570 Fruitland Avenue
Maywood, OR 97119

Dear Mr. Smith:

I am applying for the draftsperson position advertised by Republic Engineering. My resume is enclosed. As you will notice, my background is very solid, just what Republic Engineering needs.

Another thing you will notice, Mr. Smith, is the loyalty I extend toward my employer. I have twice been selected as employee of the month. Republic Engineering is surely interested in such quality.

I look forward to hearing from you concerning an interview date and time. In the meanwhile, could you provide me with a copy of your annual report? Thank you.

Sincerely,

Michael Gregory

Encl.

You just found out that Mr. Smith is no longer with Republic Engineering. The letter has to be sent to Ms. Matthews.

1. Choose **Replace** from the **Search** menu.

   The dialog box as shown in Figure 4-5 appears.

2. Type **Mr. Smith** and press [Tab].
3. Type **Ms. Matthews**.

If you click the **Find Next** button, the first occurrence of "Mr. Smith" will be replaced by "Ms. Matthews." However, if you click the **Replace All** button, all occurrences of "Mr. Smith" will be replaced by "Ms. Matthews."

Figure 4-5

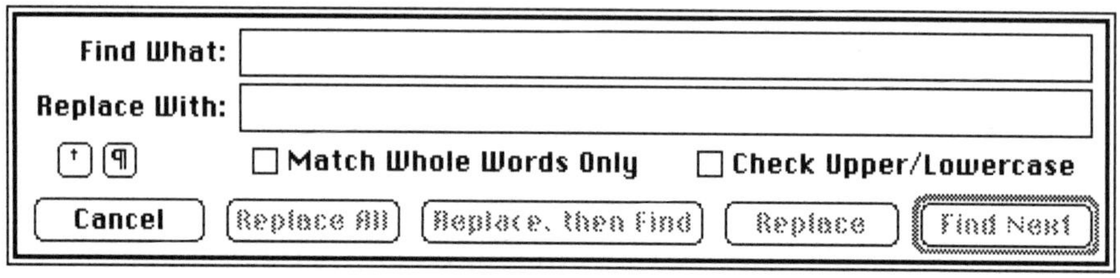

4. Click on the **Replace All** button.

   All occurrences have been replaced.

5. Click on **OK**.

PRACTICE TIME

1. Replace all occurrences of "Republic Engineering" with "Conway Architects."
2. Save the letter as LETTER 3.
3. Close the file LETTER 3.

PAGING

When you have a long, multiple-page document, Works shows you where the printer will advance to a new page. These are known as **soft page breaks** and are shown as a horizontal dotted line on the screen. As you look over the document, you may find that a soft page break will occur at some inappropriate place. For example, you do not want a page break to occur after printing just one line of a paragraph or in the middle of a table. In such a case you need to enter a page break manually, known as a **hard page break**. A hard page break is inserted by positioning the insertion bar where you want the page break to occur and choosing Insert Page Break from the Format menu.

1. Make sure that My File is displayed.
2. Position the insertion bar on the blank line between two paragraphs.
3. Choose **Insert Page Break** from the **Format** menu.

   A horizontal dotted line indicating a hard page break appears.

4. Print My File.

   The two paragraphs are printed on separate pages.

PAGE NUMBERING

When you are creating a multiple-page document, you may want to print the page number on each page. The page number can be specified as a footer or header depending on where you want it printed. The following formatting commands are available in entering a footer or header:

&l Align the following characters at the left margin.

&c Center the following characters.

&r Align the following characters at the right margin.

&d Print the current date.

&p Print the page number.

&b Print the following characters in bold.

Let's say that you want a page number to appear centered at the bottom of the page. Entering &c tells Works to center the footer text. Entering &p tells Works to print the page number. So, you will enter &c&p.

1. Choose **Page Setup** from the **File** menu.
2. Press [Tab] so that the insertion bar is on **Footer**.
3. Type **&c&p**.
4. Click the **OK** button.
5. Print the file again.

   The page numbers are printed.

This is the end of this lesson. Quit Works as described in Lesson One. There is no need to save any changes to files.

■ *SUMMARY*

Topic or Feature	*Command or Reference*	*Menu*	*Page*
Move or Copy Text to Another Document	Select text		39
	Cut/Copy	Edit	
	Choose another document	Window	

Topic or Feature	*Command or Reference*	*Menu*	*Page*
	Position insertion bar		
	Paste	Edit	
Justification	Justification	Format	40
Set Tab	Pointer on the Ruler Line where tab is to be set		42
Right Tab	Click twice		
Left Tab	Click once		
Decimal Tab	Click three times		
Find Text	Find	Search	43
Find and Replace Text	Replace	Search	44
Paging	Insert Page Break	Format	46
Page Numbering	Page Setup	File	47

■ SELF-TEST

1. To move or copy text from one document to another, you place the text on the ____________________.
2. After you paste information from the Clipboard, the information ____________________ (is/is not) erased from the Clipboard.
3. When you enter text right justified, it appears aligned with the ____________________ margin.
4. If you click the mouse twice while setting the tab, the tab is set as a ____________________ tab.
5. A decimal tab aligns the entry at ____________________.
6. If you want to find a word (rather than a group of characters) in a document, you click on the ____________________ option in the Find command.
7. If you want Works to automatically replace all occurrences of a word with another word, you click on the ____________________ option in the Replace command.

8. On a long document, Works automatically marks locations where the printer will advance to a new page. These marks are called ______________________________.

9. To manually insert a page break, choose ______________ from the ______________ menu.

10. To insert page numbers at the bottom center of a document, you enter &c&p in the ______________________________.

LESSON FIVE

Spreadsheet: Creating a Simple Spreadsheet

OBJECTIVES

In this lesson you will learn how to:

- Use spreadsheet terminology.
- Create a spreadsheet file on the desktop.
- Select cells.
- Enter data into a spreadsheet file.
- Differentiate between text and number entries.
- Enter simple formulas.
- Save a file on a disk.
- Print a spreadsheet.

First, your computer must be started and the Works program launched. Follow the instructions given in Lesson One so that the Open dialog box is displayed.

CREATING A SPREADSHEET FILE

To create a spreadsheet file:

1. Click on the Spreadsheet application icon.
2. Click on the **New** button.

   An empty spreadsheet screen as shown in Figure 5-1 (on the following page) is displayed.

At the top of the screen is the spreadsheet Menu Bar. In the middle of the Title Bar, the file name, Untitled, appears, along with (SS) to show the part of Works you are currently using.

The worksheet is divided into rows and columns. Rows are numbered (1, 2, 3, and so on), and columns are lettered (A, B, C, and so on). Each intersection of a row and a column (A1, B3, C17) is referred to as a **cell**.

Figure 5-1

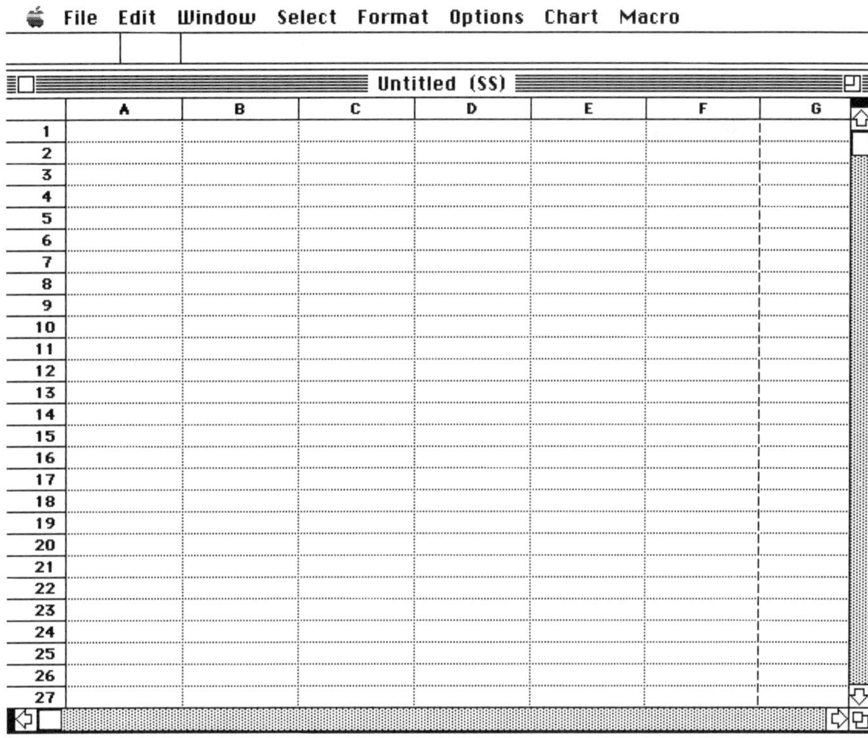

ACTIVE CELL

Before you can enter data in a cell, the cell must be selected. The selected cell is called the **active cell**. The line below the Menu Bar is called the **entry bar**. The first box of the entry bar, called the **cell indicator**, displays the coordinate of the active cell, and the third box displays the content of the active cell.

Select cell A1 by positioning the pointer on the cell and clicking the mouse.

A box appears around cell A1 as shown in Figure 5-2.

The cell indicator shows the coordinate of the active cell.

Figure 5-2

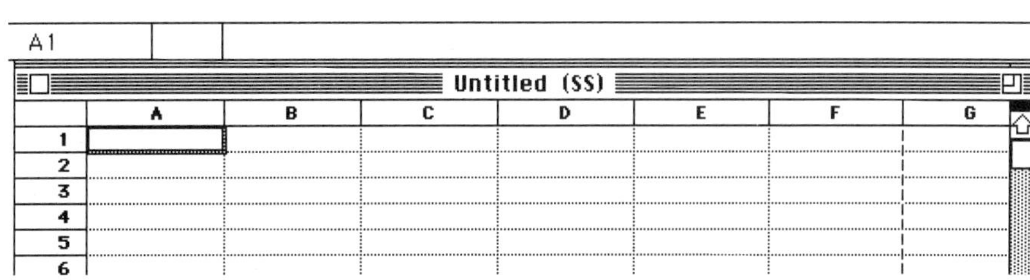

If there already was an entry in the active cell, the third box on the entry bar would display the content.

PRACTICE TIME

Select various cells to make them active. Then select cell A1.

SPREADSHEET SIZE

Click several times on the down arrow of the vertical Scroll Bar. Then click several times on the right arrow of the horizontal Scroll Bar. Notice that the column and row headings change. The worksheet doesn't contain just 6 columns and 17 rows. There are 256 columns labeled A, B, C . . . , X, Y, Z, AA, AB, AC . . . , and there are 16,382 rows. Because of the space limitation imposed by your screen, however, you can see only so many rows and columns at any one time.

NOTE: The number of columns displayed depends on the column width.

FINDING A CELL

Suppose you want to select a particular cell to make it active, and this cell is not currently displayed on the screen. You can use the Find Cell command to locate it.

1. Choose **Find Cell** from the **Select** menu.

   A dialog box as shown in Figure 5-3 is displayed.

2. Enter a cell coordinate, say **H21**, that you want to make active.

Figure 5-3

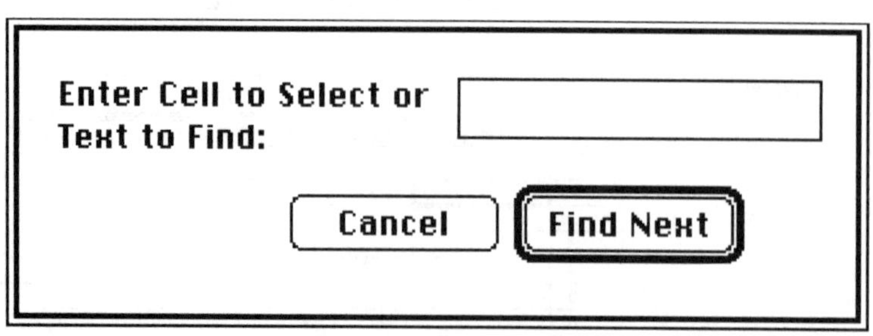

3. Click on the **Find Next** button.

   The cell H21 appears on the screen and has been made active.

PRACTICE TIME

1. Make cell C75 active.
2. Make cell F23 active.
3. When you are satisfied that you can make any cell active, select cell A1 again.

ENTERING DATA

The data you enter at a cell is text, a number, or a formula. A **text entry** is a combination of character(s) or word(s) and is not used in calculations. An example of text entry is a heading, known as a **label**, that is needed so you can later identify what other entries on the same row or column stand for. **Number entries** are values that can be used for calculations. Text entries are displayed left justified and numbers are displayed right justified in the cell. **Formula entries** will be discussed a little later, but they are entries which, when evaluated, yield the numbers that are displayed in their cells.

Text and numbers are known as **constant values**. To enter a constant value, you select a cell and type the entry. Works determines an entry as a text or a number by the first character you enter.

- If the first character is a letter (A to Z), Works assumes that you are entering text.
- If the first character is a digit (0 to 9), a decimal point, a plus (+) or minus (–) sign, or another special character (special characters will not be discussed here), the program assumes you are typing in a number.

NOTE: If you want to begin a text entry with a number, type a quotation mark (") first, then enter the text. The quotation mark is a signal to Works that you're typing text. The mark appears in the entry bar, but not in the cell.

Uppercase. To make an uppercase character in your text entry, hold Shift down while you press the character, just as you would on a typewriter. If you want to type the entire entry in uppercase letters, press Caps Lock into the down position. To type lowercase letters again, press Caps Lock again so that it is in the up position. When entering special characters (nonalphabetic characters that require the use of the shift key), you need to hold Shift down even if Caps Lock is in the down position.

As you type the entry, it appears in the entry bar. If you notice an error, you can press Backspace to back up and make corrections. When you finish typing the entry, you should visually verify the entry as displayed on the entry bar before completing the entry. Methods of completing the entry are discussed in a while.

PREPARING THE WORKSHEET

You will learn the various features of a Microsoft Works spreadsheet through an example. You will help Susan, who has started a new business and wants to keep track of her income and expenses using a spreadsheet. She wants to find out what her profit is each day.

You will start by setting up the worksheet for just the first day In the next two lessons, you will add more entries and expand and modify the worksheet.

ENTERING TEXT

First, you will label the rows by making text entries that explain what data are entered in the rows. You will use the labels "Income," "Expense," and "Profit." If the label you are entering is too long to fit in one cell, Microsoft Works automatically runs the label into blank adjacent cells.

1. Select cell A1.
2. Type the word **Income** (do not press Return).

   What you type appears on the entry bar as shown in Figure 5-4 on the following page.

   Notice the two check boxes on the entry bar. The box on the left with an X in it is the **cancel box**. The one on the right with a check in it is the **enter box**. You click on the enter box to complete the entry. If you decide against making the entry, you can cancel by clicking on the cancel box.
3. Click on the enter box.

   The word "Income" appears at cell A1, left justified.

Figure 5-4

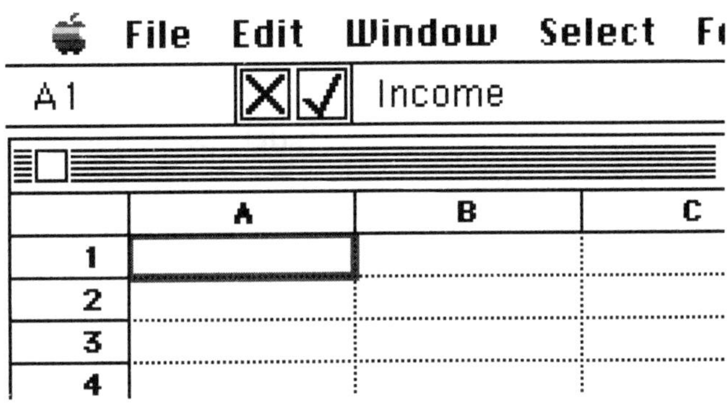

Correcting Errors

We all make errors. If you notice an error after completing an entry, you can do one of the following to correct it:

- You can reenter the entry by selecting the cell containing the error and then reentering the correct data.
- If you made an entry in a wrong cell, you can erase the entry by using the Clear command. That is, select the cell to be erased, then choose **Clear** from the **Edit** menu.

Select cell A2, type the label **Expense**, and click on the enter box.

NOTE: You can complete an entry by pressing other keys as well. If you press [Return]*, the entry is made; then the cell below becomes active. In a similar manner, completing with* [Tab] *makes the cell on the right active;* [Shift]-[Tab] *makes the cell on the left active;* [Shift]-[Return] *makes the cell above active; and* [Enter] *on the numeric keypad leaves the same cell active.*

PRACTICE TIME

1. Enter the label **Profit** at cell A3.
2. Select cell B1.

ENTERING NUMBERS

Susan earns $600 the first day, and she spends $400 in advertising expenses. Enter these values in the worksheet.

1. With cell B1 selected, type the value **600**.
2. Click on the enter box.

   The number 600 appears right justified in cell B1.
3. Select cell B2.
4. Enter the value **400** in cell B2.

ENTERING FORMULAS

Instead of entering a number in cell B3, you will enter a formula that will cause the computer to calculate the profit. The formula is "income minus expense." That is, the formula determines the difference between the numbers stored in cells B1 and B2, or B1 minus B2. The result is displayed in cell B3.

A formula entry is indicated by an equals sign (=) as the first character in the entry. When you enter a formula, the formula itself appears in the entry bar as the content of the cell. The cell, however, displays the numeric result after the formula is evaluated.

In a formula, the operator + is used to indicate addition, – to indicate subtraction, * to indicate multiplication, and / to indicate division. These operators are evaluated from left to right. As in ordinary mathematics, multiplication and division take precedence over addition and subtraction unless the latter operations are enclosed in parentheses. Example: =6+4/2 will result in 8, whereas =(6+4)/2 equals 5.

Let's return to helping Susan start her business. The formula for Profit is =B1–B2.

1. Select cell B3, type =B1–B2, then click on the enter box.

   The entry bar shows the content as =B1–B2.

   Cell B3 shows the number 200, which is the result of evaluating the formula (600-400).
2. In cell B2, enter any number other than 400, for instance, 250.

   Did you notice what happened to the number at B3? If you missed it, enter another number at cell B2. The number in B3 changes.

The computer saves the formula for the value displayed at B3. This cell always displays the result of the expression =B1–B2. Thus, the computer recalculates B3 every time you change the values in B1 or B2.

Are you beginning to see the power of a spreadsheet?

As you entered this formula, you may have had to check for the coordinates of cells displaying the values for income and expenses. Had this been a large spreadsheet, you may have had trouble determining which cell contains which value. If the cells you wanted had scrolled off the window, you would have had to scroll the window to find them. After finding them, you would have had to note their position, select the cell in which you wanted to enter the formula, and then type the formula. The spreadsheet program can make this process a little easier.

1. Clear the entry at cell B3 by choosing cell B3 then selecting **Clear** from the **Edit** menu.

   Cell B3 clears.

Now, to enter the formula,

2. Press the = key (do not press Return).

   = appears on the entry bar.

3. Click on cell B1 where the value for income appears.

   The entry bar now reads =B1.

4. Press the – key.

   The entry bar reads =B1–.

Now, enter the second part of the formula by clicking on the cell that contains the value for expense.

5. Click on cell B2 where the value for the expense appears.

   The entry bar now reads =B1–B2.

6. Click on the enter box.

You can see that clicking on cells has the same results as typing those cell coordinates directly from the keyboard.

7. Enter the value **400** at B2.

PRACTICE TIME

1. Susan decides that 25 percent of her profit should go toward purchasing new equipment. Enter the label **Equipment** in cell A4. In cell B4, enter a formula for evaluating the amount to be spent on equipment. The formula is .25 of the value in cell B3, or **=.25*B3**.

2. Susan wants to know her net profit after purchasing equipment. Enter in row 5 the label **-Net-** and the formula used to calculate it. The formula for net is profit minus equipment, or **=B3–B4**. (See Figure 5-5.)

Figure 5-5

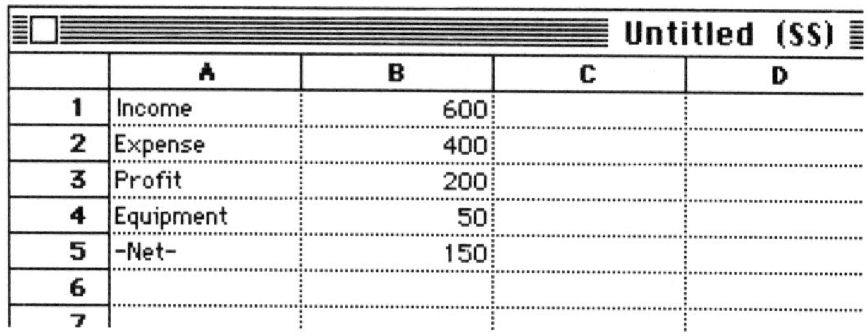

Untitled (SS)

	A	B	C	D
1	Income	600		
2	Expense	400		
3	Profit	200		
4	Equipment	50		
5	-Net-	150		
6				
7				

SAVING YOUR WORK

The spreadsheet you see in front of you is sitting on the desktop, which is the RAM of the computer. When you turn the computer off, all the information will be gone. Usually, you develop a worksheet in one or more sessions and then use it again in subsequent sessions. Thus, it is important to save the worksheet in more permanent storage.

You will use the name MONEY to save the spreadsheet on the data disk.

1. Insert your data disk in the drive.
2. Choose **Save As** from the **File** menu.

   The Save As dialog box appears, with the original name Untitled selected.
3. Type **MONEY**.

   MONEY replaces Untitled.
4. Make sure that the correct drive is selected for your data disk.
5. Click on the **Save** button.

   Works saves the spreadsheet as a new file on the disk and changes the name on the Title Bar.

   You return to the spreadsheet.

PRINTING THE SPREADSHEET

Now, print the spreadsheet using the Print command.

1. Make sure that the printer is turned on and is ready for use.
2. Choose **Print** from the **File** menu.

   The Print dialog box similar to the ones shown in Figures 5-6(a) and 5-6(b) is displayed.

Figure 5-6(a)

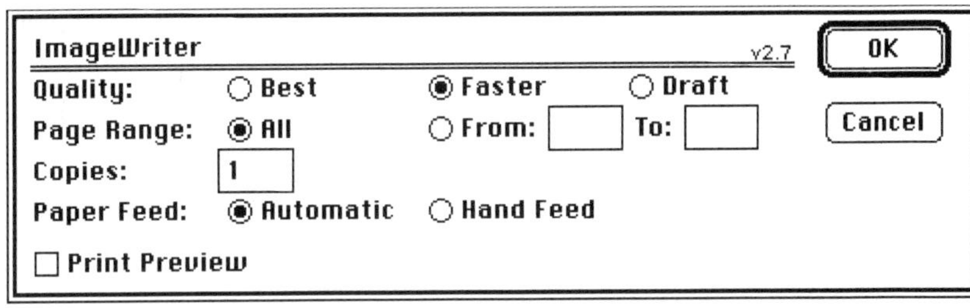

Figure 5-6(b)

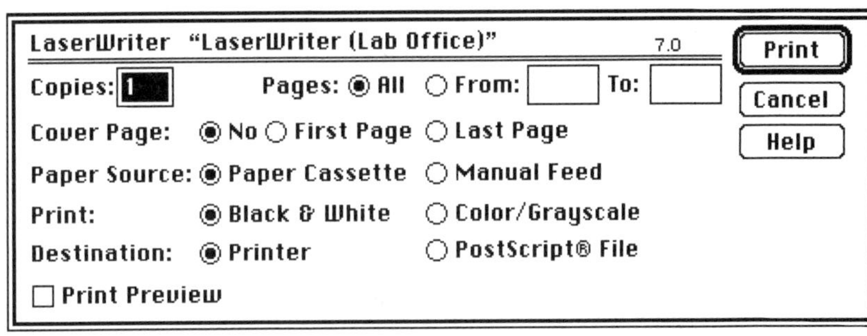

3. Change options, if needed.
4. Click the **OK** or **Print** button.

   Your spreadsheet is printed.

NOTE: If you want to cancel printing, hold down ⌘ and type a period.

If your printout looks good, you are done with this lesson. If it doesn't, go back and fix your spreadsheet. After you make corrections, save your work using the Save command and print it again.

This is the end of this lesson. Quit Works as described in Lesson One.

■ SUMMARY

Topic or Feature	*Command or Reference*	*Menu*	*Page*
Select a Cell	Point and click		51
Find a Cell	Find Cell	Select	52
Enter Text	Entry that starts with A-Z or a quotation mark (")		54
Enter Numbers	Entry that starts with a number, a decimal point, a plus (+) or minus (–) sign		55

Topic or Feature	*Command or Reference*	*Menu*	*Page*
Enter Formulas	Entry that starts with an equals sign (=)		56
Erase an Entry	Clear	Edit	57
Save a Spreadsheet	Save or Save As	File	58
Print a Spreadsheet	Print	File	58

■ SELF-TEST

1. The selected cell is called the ______________________ cell.
2. A particular cell can be selected without scrolling through the whole spreadsheet by choosing the ____________ from the __________ menu.
3. An entry can be completed by ____.
4. Microsoft Works assumes an entry to be text when it starts with ____.
5. Miscrosoft determines an entry to be a formula when it starts with a(n) ____.
6. The symbol used to indicate multiplication in a formula is __________.
7. If the formula entered is =2+8/4, the value displayed at the cell is ____.
8. The cell address in a formula can be entered by __________ and clicking on the referenced cell.
9. You clear an entry in a cell by selecting the cell and choosing the ____________ command from the ____________ menu.
10. To print a spreadsheet, you choose the __________ command from the __________ menu.

LESSON SIX

Spreadsheet: Expanding and Formatting the Simple Spreadsheet

OBJECTIVES

In this lesson you will learn how to:

- Retrieve a spreadsheet file from a disk.
- Insert a row.
- Change column width.
- Use a function.
- Specify a range reference.
- Save a file using a different filename.
- Print a spreadsheet in a horizontal orientation.

Your Macintosh should be started and the Works program launched so that the Open dialog box is displayed. Make sure that you have the data disk from Lesson Five in the drive.

First you will retrieve the spreadsheet from the last lesson.

1. Click on the Spreadsheet application icon.
2. Make sure that the drive for your data disk has been selected.
3. Select the file MONEY in the list box, and click on the **Open** button.

   The spreadsheet from the previous lesson is displayed on the screen.

INSERT COMMAND

Right now, your worksheet shows values for Income, Expense, Profit, Equipment, and Net for one day. You will now extend these entries to show 10 days of business activity. You will enter the figures for the second day in column C, for the third day in column D, and so on. To identify the values easily, you will enter headings for these columns.

The column headings should go on row 1. Do you see a problem? Row 1 already has some entries. You could erase the whole spreadsheet and start over again, putting Income in row 2, Expense in row 3, Profit in row 4, and so on. However, there is an easier way. You can insert a row at row 1.

1. Select row 1 by positioning the pointer on the row heading 1 and clicking the mouse button.

   Row 1 is selected as displayed in Figure 6-1.

Figure 6-1

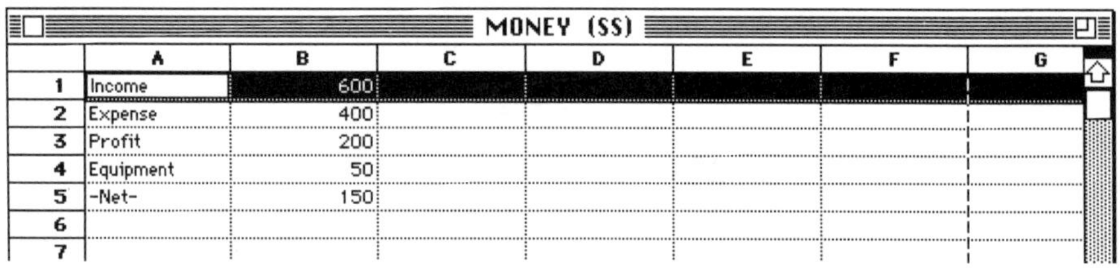

2. Choose **Insert** from the **Edit** menu.

   All the information on the spreadsheet moves down one row, and row 1 is now blank.

Let's proceed with labeling the columns.

3. Select cell A1 and enter the label **Day**.
4. Select cell B1 and enter **1**.

Now, you need to enter 2 at C1, 3 at D1 . . . , 10 at K1. To do this, you select cell C1 and enter 2, select cell D1 and enter 3, and so on. But try a different way. Each entry is 1 greater than the previous one. The entry in C1 is the entry in B1 plus 1; the entry in D1 is the entry in C1 plus 1; and so on. So, you can enter the formula =B1+1 at C1, =C1+1 at D1, and so on.

5. Select cell C1 and enter **=B1+1**.

   The number 2 is displayed at C1.

Now, think for a moment. You will have to enter the formula =C1+1 at cell D1, =D1+1 at cell E1, and so on up to =J1+1 at K1. How tedious to enter nearly the same formula over and over. In this case, you need to do this only nine times. But what if you were setting up the worksheet for a month or a year?

FILL RIGHT COMMAND

There is an easier way: use the Fill Right command from the Edit menu. You can use this command to make copies of formulas, texts, numbers, or blank entries across a row.

1. Drag the mouse to select cells C1 through K1.
2. Select **Fill Right** from the **Edit** menu.

   Numbers appear in columns D through K as shown in Figure 6-2.

Figure 6-2

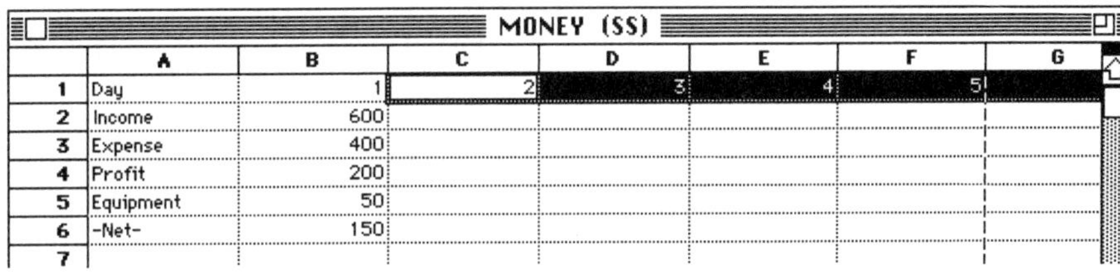

3. Select cells along row 1. Notice the contents of each cell as displayed on the entry bar.

As the formula =B1+1 was copied to cells D1 through K1, the cell coordinate changed for each cell. The formula is =B1+1 in cell C1, =C1+1 in cell D1, and so on just as you wanted. The formula =B1+1 gave a **relative reference** for the cell address rather than an **absolute reference**. A relative reference gives general directions to Works. In this case, the formula simply said add 1 to the content of the cell to the left and display the result. That was the formula that was copied all the way across. An absolute reference would have given the specific cell coordinate. To give an absolute reference, you enter the formula with a dollar sign ($) preceding the cell's column label and row number. For example, if you wanted the formula =B1+1 to appear in all the cells, you would enter B1+1.

CHANGE COLUMN WIDTH

Initially, every column in the spreadsheet is 12 characters wide; that is, 12 characters are displayed at each coordinate. You can change the column width to up to 40 characters.

You change the width of a column either by choosing Column Width from the Format menu or by dragging the right edge of the column heading. You can change the width of multiple columns by using the first method. You will now change the column width of columns A through K.

1. Select columns A through K by clicking and dragging the mouse on the headings for columns A through K.

2. Choose **Column Width** from the **Format** menu.

   The dialog box as shown in Figure 6-3 appears.

Figure 6-3

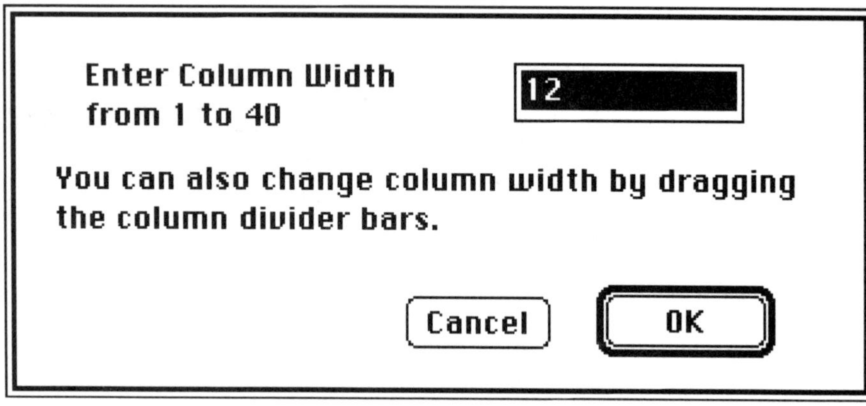

You will change the column width of columns A through K to 7.

3. Type **7** and click on the **OK** button.

   The width for columns A through K changes to 7.

The width of a single column can be changed by following the steps just described. Right now, however, you will use another method to change the width of column A.

1. Place the pointer on the column heading, on the line between columns A and B.

   The pointer turns into a cross.

2. Click on the mouse and drag to the right. Don't release the mouse button.

   Notice the dotted line move to the right.

3. When the dotted line is positioned where you want the right edge of the column to be, release the mouse button.

   The column width is set.

When you set the column width in this manner, however, you cannot readily tell the exact character width of the column.

NOTE: When you change the width of a column, the value or the text stored is not affected. The change affects only the number of characters displayed on the spreadsheet. If a value stored in the cell is too large to be displayed within the specified column width, the cell will be filled with number signs (#). If a text stored in the cell is too long to be displayed within the specified column width, Works automatically runs the label in blank adjacent cells.

Make sure that the width of column A is set to 11.

PRACTICE TIME

1. Decrease the width of column B to 2. Notice that cells B2, B3, B4, and B6 fill with number signs.
2. Change the width of column B to 7.
3. Enter the following values for days 2 through 5.

Day	2	3	4	5
Income	**300**	**950**	**1000**	**692.50**
Expense	**275**	**500**	**500**	**600.34**

4. Copy the formulas for Profit, Equipment, and Net, as entered in cells B4, B5, and B6, into the range C4 through K4, C5 through K5, and C6 through K6, respectively. (See Figure 6-4.)

Figure 6-4

MONEY (SS)

	A	B	C	D	E	F	G	H	I	J
1	Day	1	2	3	4	5	6	7	8	9
2	Income	600	300	950	1000	692.5				
3	Expense	400	275	500	500	600.34				
4	Profit	200	25	450	500	92.1600	0	0	0	0
5	Equipment	50	6.25	112.5	125	23.04	0	0	0	0
6	-Net-	150	18.75	337.5	375	69.1200	0	0	0	0
7										
8										
9										

Now, Susan can see the profitability of the business at a glance. Columns G through K are blank for Income and Expense rows and show zero (0) for the rest. These columns are already set up so that as Susan enters values for income and expense on days 6 through 10, profit, equipment, and net will be calculated and displayed automatically.

NOTE: It is possible to set up an entire spreadsheet without data. It can contain all the headings and formulas needed, have all columns set to the proper width, and have the display format specified. Such a spreadsheet is called a ***template****. A template is a prewritten spreadsheet that is ready to accept data. To utilize a template, just retrieve it and enter data into the proper cells.*

It occurs to Susan at this point that she started the business with a certain amount of cash. Call it cash-on-hand. She would like to see the change in that value from day to day. She decides that she would like to see this figure on row 2.

PRACTICE TIME

1. Insert a blank row at row 2.
2. Enter the row heading **Cash-on-Hand** in cell A2.
3. If needed, adjust the width of column A so that the heading fits.
4. Enter the value **750** in cell B2 as the starting value.

   Your screen should look similar to Figure 6-5.

Figure 6-5

	A	B	C	D	
1	Day	1	2	3	
2	Cash-on-Hand	750			
3	Income	600	300	950	
4	Expense	400	275	500	
5	Profit	200	25	450	
6	Equipment	50	6.25	112.5	
7	-Net-	150	18.75	337.5	

Think about this for a minute. The value for cash-on-hand changes daily depending on the net profit. On the second day the cash-on-hand is the sum of the cash-on-hand for the first day plus the net profit for the first day. So the formula used for cash-on-hand for the second day is the value at cell B2 plus the value at cell B7.

PRACTICE TIME

1. Enter the formula for cash-on-hand for the second day.
2. Copy this formula to the range D2 through K2 as shown in Figure 6-6.

Figure 6-6

MONEY (SS)

	A	B	C	D	E	F	G	H	I	J
1	Day	1	2	3	4	5	6	7	8	9
2	Cash-on-Hand	750	900	918.75	1256.25	1631.25	1700.37	1700.37	1700.37	1700.37
3	Income	600	300	950	1000	692.5				
4	Expense	400	275	500	500	600.34				
5	Profit	200	25	450	500	92.1600	0	0	0	0
6	Equipment	50	6.25	112.5	125	23.04	0	0	0	0
7	-Net-	150	18.75	337.5	375	69.1200	0	0	0	0
8										

Cash-on-hand values for days 6 through 10 remain constant since net values are zero for those days.

SUM FUNCTION

For column L, Susan decides that she would like to see totals for income, expense, profit, equipment, and net for the 10-day period. To enter the total income at L3, for instance, you could enter the formula =B3+C3+D3+E3+F3+G3+H3+I3+J3+K3. That's a long formula. Suppose you had to find the total income for 60 days? As you might have guessed, there is an easier way to total numbers. You can use the Sum function.

A function is a built-in calculation. A Sum function will give you the sum of things you specify, called **arguments**. The arguments can be:

- A number—a specific value, such as 5 or 246.
- A formula—an expression that gives a number, when evaluated, such as 8/3.
- A cell reference—the coordinate of a cell whose content you want added such as A17 or G92.
- A range reference—coordinates of a range of cells whose contents you want added. A range is a rectangular section of a spreadsheet. You reference a range by specifying the coordinates of top left and bottom right corner cells of the range, separated by a colon (:), for example, A7:A15 or C1:E5.
- Another function.

1. Select cell L3.
2. Choose **Paste Function** from the **Edit** menu.

   The Paste Function dialog box appears as shown in Figure 6-7.

Works has 64 built-in functions that you can either paste or type into a spreadsheet. Some functions require arguments. Others do not. Right now, you want to use the Sum function.

Figure 6-7

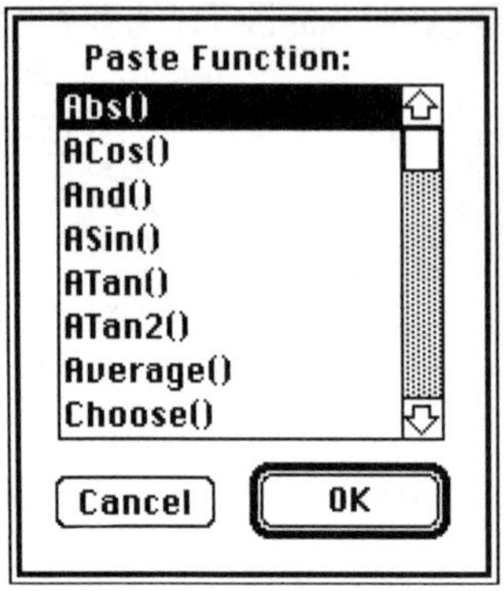

3. Scroll the list box until **Sum()** appears.
4. Select **Sum()** and click on the **OK** box.

   =Sum() appears on the entry bar with the insertion bar positioned between the parentheses.

You are now to indicate what values you want totaled. That is, you are to specify the arguments. In this case, you want to enter a range reference. You want to total the values on row 3, columns B to K.

5. Type **B3:K3** and complete the entry.

   In cell L3, the value 3542.5 appears.

You could have specified the range using the mouse, by selecting cells B3 through K3.

NOTE: Functions and arguments may also be typed in. Make certain the function name is preceded by an equals (=) sign.

PRACTICE TIME

1. Copy the formula in L3 to cells L4 through L7.

   Hint: Select cells L3 through L7, then select **Fill Down** from the **Edit** menu.

2. Enter the label **TOTAL** in cell L1.

SAVING A FILE USING A DIFFERENT FILENAME

Save your spreadsheet for use during the next lesson. When you are saving the spreadsheet, however, you have to be careful in choosing the filename.

If you use the same filename you did at the end of the last lesson, the current spreadsheet will replace the existing contents of the disk file. This may be acceptable in some situations. By using a different filename, however, both the old and new spreadsheets will be stored on the disk. As you learned in Lesson One, you use the Save As command to save the spreadsheet with a different name.

You will save the spreadsheet using a different filename since the spreadsheets from this and Lesson Five will be used in the next lesson.

1. Choose **Save As** from the **File** menu.

   The Save As dialog box appears, with the original name MONEY displayed.

2. Type **MONEY 2**.

   MONEY 2 replaces MONEY.

3. Make sure that the correct drive is selected for your data disk.

4. Click on the **Save** button.

   The current spreadsheet is saved on the disk.

   You return to the spreadsheet.

PRACTICE TIME

Print the spreadsheet by choosing Print from the File menu. Do not change any options; just click on the OK button. You will notice that the spreadsheet is printed on two sheets since the entire spreadsheet could not be printed on one page. A vertical dotted line on the spreadsheet indicates the location of the right margin.

PRINTING THE SPREADSHEET WITH HORIZONTAL ORIENTATION

Your printout cannot be any wider than the paper width specified through the Page Setup option.

1. Choose **Page Setup** from the **File** menu.

   The Page Setup dialog box is displayed.

The Page Setup command lets you specify paper size, printing orientation, special effects, headers, footers, and margins. These settings will affect the appearance of the printed spreadsheet. To change the settings, click on the appropriate options.

Notice that by default the paper selected is a standard (U.S. letter) 8½″ by 11″. Also, the orientation is set to vertical. That means the spreadsheet is printed on an 8½-inch-wide paper. If the spreadsheet requires more columns than can be printed on 8½-inch width (with 1-inch margin on each side), it will be printed on multiple pages. There are several options you can use to print more columns on a single sheet, such as reducing the size of the print, using different size characters, using larger paper, reducing margins, or changing the printing orientation.

Now you will change the orientation so that the spreadsheet is printed sideways. This will allow for a spreadsheet to print on the 11-inch width instead.

1. Click on the sideways image under the heading **Orientation**. This is the horizontal orientation.
2. Click on the **OK** button.
3. Print the spreadsheet again without changing any options.

   The spreadsheet is printed sideways. More columns are printed on a sheet.

NOTE: *Whether the entire spreadsheet is printed on one sheet or not will depend on the printer you are using and whether or not your column widths were set to the same values as the example in the lesson.*

This is the end of this lesson. Quit Works as described in Lesson One.

■ SUMMARY

Topic or Feature	*Command or Reference*	*Menu*	*Page*
Insert a Row	Select row(s)		62
	Insert	Edit	
Copy a Cell Content Across a Row	Select cells in a row, including the one whose content you want to copy		62
	Fill Right	Edit	
Change Column Width	Select column(s)		63
	Column Width	Format	
	or		
	Point to the right edge of the column heading		
	Drag the mouse		
Use Functions	Paste Function	Edit	67

Topic or Feature	*Command or Reference*	*Menu*	*Page*
Change Printing Orientation	Page Setup	File	69

■ SELF-TEST

1. If you used a relative reference to copy the formula =A1+A2 in cell B1 to cell C1, the content of cell C1 is ______________________.
2. If a cell is not wide enough to show a number, the cell displays ______________________.
3. You can change the width of a column by positioning the pointer on ______________________ and dragging.
4. You can change the width of any number of columns by selecting those columns and choosing the ______________ command from the ________ menu.
5. To copy a cell content to selected cells along the same row, you highlight all cells, including the one whose content you want to copy, and select the ______________ command from the ______________ menu.
6. If a cell is to contain the formula =B1+C1+C2+C3, it can be entered (using a function) as ______________________.
7. Function names can be pasted into a formula by choosing the ______________ command from the Edit menu.
8. In the formula entry =Sum(A1:A4), ______________ is the argument.
9. When you save a file the second time using the same filename, the original file is ______________________.
10. When you print a spreadsheet on an 8½" by 11" paper with horizontal orientation, it is printed on ______________-inch-wide paper.

LESSON SEVEN

Spreadsheet: Modifying the Display Format

OBJECTIVES

In this lesson you will learn how to:

- Change the display format of the entire worksheet or just the selected cells.
- Move information within the worksheet.
- Delete columns.
- Display formulas that were entered in the worksheet.
- Cut and paste information from one spreadsheet to another.
- Sort rows in a spreadsheet.

Your Macintosh should be started and the Works program launched so that the Open dialog box is displayed. Make sure that you have the data disk from Lesson Six in the drive and retrieve the spreadsheet file, MONEY 2.

CHANGE DISPLAY FORMAT

You can improve the readability of a spreadsheet by changing the display format. You can change the format of the entire worksheet or of selected cells. This is done by selecting either the entire spreadsheet or cell(s) and using the Set Cell Attributes command from the Format menu.

Bold Characters

Headings on the spreadsheet can be made to stand out by displaying them in bold characters.

1. Drag the mouse to select cells A1 through L1.

2. Select **Set Cell Attributes** from the **Format** menu.

   The dialog box as displayed in Figure 7-1 appears.

Figure 7-1

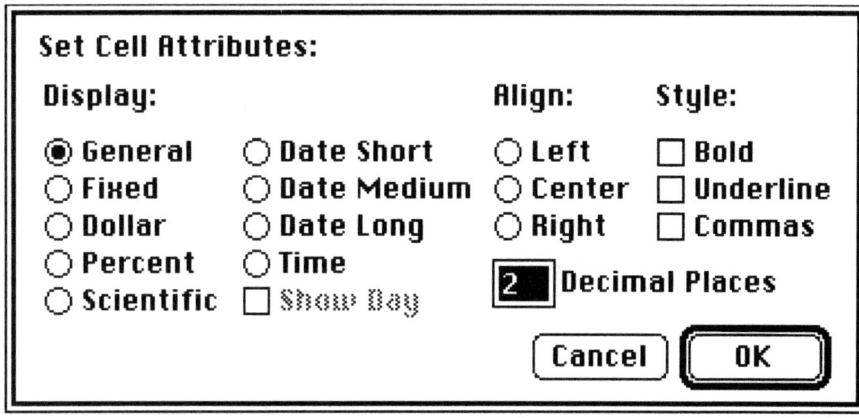

This dialog box shows various display options. Select the proper option and click on the OK button. Style options are displayed on the rightmost column.

3. Click on the **Bold** box.

   An X appears in the box.

4. Click on the **OK** button.

   The column headings are now displayed in bold characters.

To change the style back to normal, go through the same procedure. This time, the X disappears from the box. The buttons in the cell attributes dialog box are **toggle switches**. The feature turns on or off each time you select it.

PRACTICE TIME

Change the display of row headings in column A to bold.

Justifying Text Entry

Does anything about the column heading TOTAL bother you? It doesn't line up above all the values for the totals. The reason is that values are displayed right justified, whereas texts are displayed left justified in the spreadsheet. You can change the text format for this cell alone so that it is right justified.

1. Make sure the cell L1 is selected.
2. Choose **Set Cell Attributes** from the **Format** menu.

   On the third column, various alignment options are displayed.
3. Click on **Right**, then on the **OK** button.

   The word "TOTAL" is displayed right justified at cell L1.

Display Format of Numbers

Since this spreadsheet shows dollar amounts, you probably want to change the format to show two places to the right of the decimal point. So, let's do this for the entire spreadsheet.

1. Choose **Select All** from the **Edit** menu.

   The entire spreadsheet is selected.
2. Choose **Set Cell Attributes** from the **Format** menu.

The first two columns display the various options available for display. The first column shows options for displaying numbers. Currently, the display is set to General. General format means Works will display the number as accurately as possible, given the cell width. For example, if you type 12345.6789, it may display as 12345.6789, 12345.7, 12346, 1E+4 (scientific), and so on, depending on the width of the cell.

You could use the Dollar format, but suppose that you don't want dollar signs. You can use the Fixed format with two places to the right of the decimal point.

3. Click on the **Fixed** button.

   The box to display decimal places is highlighted.
4. Type **2**, if needed, and click on the **OK** button.

   Some cells in columns E through K are filled with number signs.
5. Change the widths of columns E through K to any number greater than 7.

   All numbers are shown with two places to the right of the decimal point as displayed in Figure 7-2.

Do you see a problem? Even the column headings have two decimal places. Since these headings signify day 1, day 2, and so on, they should be whole numbers.

Figure 7-2

MONEY 2 (SS)

	A	B	C	D	E	F	G	H
1	Day	1	2	3	4	5	6	7
2	Cash-on-Hand	750.00	900.00	918.75	1256.25	1631.25	1700.37	1700.37
3	Income	600.00	300.00	950.00	1000.00	692.50		
4	Expense	400.00	275.00	500.00	500.00	600.34		
5	Profit	200.00	25.00	450.00	500.00	92.16	0.00	0.00
6	Equipment	50.00	6.25	112.50	125.00	23.04	0.00	0.00
7	-Net-	150.00	18.75	337.50	375.00	69.12	0.00	0.00
8								
9								

PRACTICE TIME

Change the display format of B1 through K1 to Fixed with zero decimal places.

CUT OR COPY AND PASTE

Susan just decided that she would like to see the values for cash-on-hand displayed as the last item on the spreadsheet, not the first. You can reenter the entries in row 2 in row 8, then remove row 2. However, it is easier to cut the entries in row 2 onto the Clipboard, then paste them on the last row.

1. Select row 2 by clicking on the row number.
2. Choose **Cut** from the **Edit** menu.

   The contents of Row 2 have been removed from the spreadsheet and placed on the Clipboard.
3. Choose **Show Clipboard** from the **Window** menu.

   The Clipboard contains the entries from row 2, as shown in Figure 7-3.

Figure 7-3

Clipboard (SS)

	A	B	C	D	E	F	G
2	Cash-on-Han	750.00	900.00	918.75	1256.25	1631.25	1700.3

4. Close the Clipboard.
5. Select row 7.
6. Choose **Paste** from the **Edit** menu.

   Cash-on-Hand appears in row 7.

NOTE: If you were to copy the entries to the Clipboard instead of cut, you would have just copied the content to the Clipboard, leaving the entries at the source intact. The Cut command, by contrast, relocates the values.

Only one piece of information can be on the Clipboard at a time. If you cut another piece of information onto the Clipboard, the previous information is replaced.

DELETING COLUMNS

Susan decided that she wants to close out her spreadsheet now. She wants to delete the columns for days 6 through 10. Columns can be deleted by cutting them.

1. Select columns G through K.
2. Choose **Cut** from the **Edit** menu.

   The screen changes to Figure 7-4.

Figure 7-4

MONEY 2 (SS)

	A	B	C	D	E	F	G	H
1	Day	1	2	3	4	5	TOTAL	
2	Income	600.00	300.00	950.00	1000.00	692.50	3542.50	
3	Expense	400.00	275.00	500.00	500.00	600.34	2275.34	
4	Profit	200.00	25.00	450.00	500.00	92.16	1267.16	
5	Equipment	50.00	6.25	112.50	125.00	23.04	316.79	
6	-Net-	150.00	18.75	337.50	375.00	69.12	950.37	
7	Cash-on-Han	750.00	750.00	750.00	750.00	750.00		
8								

3. Select cell G2.

   The entry line shows the content as =Sum(B2:F2).

Notice that the formula adjusted to accommodate deleted columns.

FORMULA DISPLAY

When you choose the Print command from the File menu, an image of what is displayed on the screen is printed on the paper. It is very difficult for someone else to tell by looking at the printout whether you entered a value or a formula to obtain the number displayed at a cell.

Even when you are looking at a spreadsheet on the screen, unless you select a particular cell (and look at the cell content), it is not possible to tell whether what is displayed is an actual value or the result of a formula.

You can have Works display what was actually entered (whether it is a value or a formula) at each cell.

Select **Show Formulas** from the **Options** menu.

A check mark appears in front of the **Show Formulas** option, and a check mark in front of the **Show Values** option disappears.

The display changes to Figure 7-5.

Figure 7-5

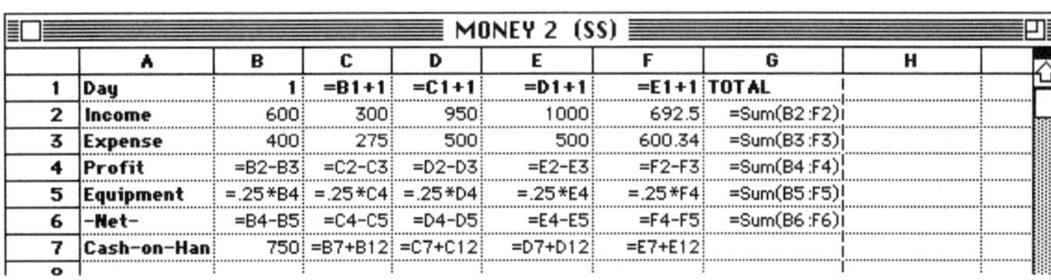

MONEY 2 (SS)

	A	B	C	D	E	F	G	H
1	Day	1	=B1+1	=C1+1	=D1+1	=E1+1	TOTAL	
2	Income	600	300	950	1000	692.5	=Sum(B2:F2)	
3	Expense	400	275	500	500	600.34	=Sum(B3:F3)	
4	Profit	=B2-B3	=C2-C3	=D2-D3	=E2-E3	=F2-F3	=Sum(B4:F4)	
5	Equipment	=.25*B4	=.25*C4	=.25*D4	=.25*E4	=.25*F4	=Sum(B5:F5)	
6	-Net-	=B4-B5	=C4-C5	=D4-D5	=E4-E5	=F4-F5	=Sum(B6:F6)	
7	Cash-on-Han	750	=B7+B12	=C7+C12	=D7+D12	=E7+E12		

NOTE: You may have to adjust the column width to accommodate formula display.

At all cells where values were entered, the entry that was typed (whether it is a number or a formula) is displayed. Look through the whole spreadsheet. You can see right away what was entered at each coordinate. You can get a printout of this formula display in the usual way.

You can also return to the regular display by choosing Show Values from the Options menu.

Choose **Show Values** from the **Options** menu.

A check mark appears in front of the **Show Values** option, and a check mark in front of the **Show Formulas** option disappears.

PRACTICE TIME

1. Change to Show Formulas display again.
2. Get a printout of formula display.

3. Change back to normal display.
4. Save the worksheet as MONEY 3.

MOVING INFORMATION BETWEEN TWO SPREADSHEETS

Sometimes you need to take information out of one spreadsheet and include it in another. In Works, information from one worksheet can be cut or copied onto the Clipboard. The information on the Clipboard can then be pasted into another worksheet.

1. Start a new spreadsheet by choosing **New** from the **File** menu. You have to then select the spreadsheet icon and click on the **OK** button.
2. In cell A1, enter text **MY BUDGET.**
3. Choose MONEY 3 from the **Window** menu.

   The spreadsheet MONEY 3 is displayed.
4. Select rows 1 to 7 by dragging on the row numbers.
5. Choose **Copy** from the **Edit** menu to copy rows 1 to 7 to the Clipboard.

As mentioned before, the information can be copied or cut onto the Clipboard. The Cut command actually removes the information from the spreadsheet and puts it on the Clipboard. When Copy is used, you only copy the information and the information still remains in the original file.

Now, you will paste the information from the Clipboard into the worksheet Untitled at cell A2.

6. Switch to Untitled.

You need to select the cell where the top left corner of the information should be positioned.

7. Select cell A2.
8. Choose **Paste** from the **Edit** menu.

   The information from the Clipboard is inserted as shown in Figure 7-6.
9. Save the spreadsheet as MY BUDGET.

SORTING ROWS

Sometimes, it is convenient if the entries in a worksheet are sorted (rearranged) so that they appear in a particular order. Suppose a spreadsheet on

Figure 7-6

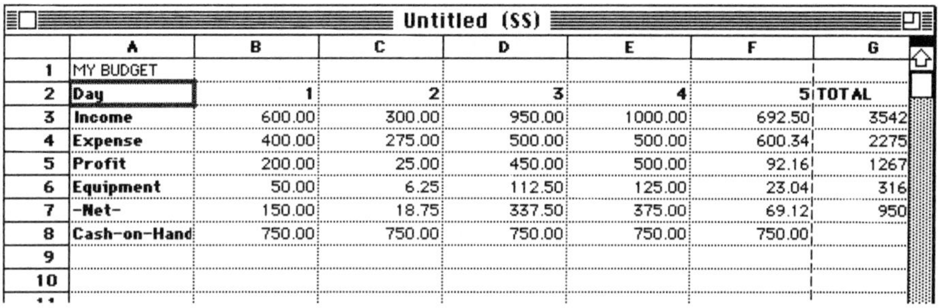

Untitled (SS)

	A	B	C	D	E	F	G
1	MY BUDGET						
2	Day	1	2	3	4	5	TOTAL
3	Income	600.00	300.00	950.00	1000.00	692.50	3542
4	Expense	400.00	275.00	500.00	500.00	600.34	2275
5	Profit	200.00	25.00	450.00	500.00	92.16	1267
6	Equipment	50.00	6.25	112.50	125.00	23.04	316
7	-Net-	150.00	18.75	337.50	375.00	69.12	950
8	Cash-on-Hand	750.00	750.00	750.00	750.00	750.00	
9							
10							

student grades currently appears in alphabetic order by last name, but you need to sort them (for printing) in order by exam scores, from highest to lowest. This can be done using the Sort command from the Edit menu.

First, you need a worksheet with data that can be sorted.

PRACTICE TIME

1. Create a new spreadsheet file and enter the following information:

	A	B	C
1	**NAME**	**I.D.**	**SCORE**
2	**Davis, P.**	**2275**	**90**
3	**Thomas, L.**	**3524**	**102**
4	**Adams, R.**	**3024**	**88**
5	**Johnson, B.**	**4001**	**92**
6	**Baker, J.**	**3026**	**98**
7	**Palmer, S.**	**1703**	**88**

2. Save the spreadsheet as SCORES.

First, you want to sort the names in alphabetic order.

1. Select the cells you want to sort. That is, select the data range A2:C7. You do not want to include the column headings.
2. Choose **Sort** from the **Edit** menu.

   The Sort dialog box is displayed as shown in Figure 7-7.

You now have to indicate the column that you want to sort by—the key column—and the sorting order (ascending or descending). In this case, it is the column containing students' last names. Since the dialog box defaults to A as the first key column and "Ascending," you don't have to change anything.

Figure 7-7

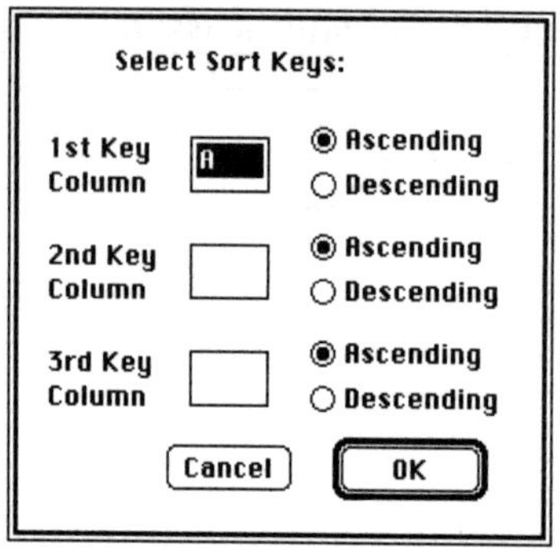

The second and third keys are used in case of a tie. For example, employees are often sorted in alphabetic order. The first key is last name, and the secondary key is first name. If two employees have the same last name, then the second key is used to break the tie. You may even want to use the middle initial as the third key. You do not have a second or third key in this case, since all last names are unique. You are ready to sort.

3. Click on the **OK** button.

   The spreadsheet is sorted.

PRACTICE TIME

1. Sort data in ascending order by I.D. numbers.
2. Sort data in descending order by scores.

This is the end of this lesson. Quit Works as discussed in Lesson One. There is no need to save any changes.

■ SUMMARY

Topic or Feature	*Command or Reference*	*Menu*	*Page*
Print in Bold	Select cells to be displayed in bold		72
	Set Cell Attributes	Format	
Format Entry	Select cells to be affected		73
	Set Cell Attributes	Format	

Topic or Feature	*Command or Reference*	*Menu*	*Page*
Select the Entire Spreadsheet	Select All	Edit	74
Move Row entry to Another Row	Select row to be moved		75
	Cut	Edit	
	Select destination row		
	Paste	Edit	
Remove Row(s) or Column(s)	Select row(s) or column(s) to be deleted		76
	Cut	Edit	
Formula Display	Show Formulas	Options	77
Move Information to Another Spreadsheet	Place information on the Clipboard		78
	Switch to another spreadsheet		
	Select cell to locate the information		
	Paste	Edit	
Arrange Rows	Select cells to sort		78
	Sort	Edit	

■ SELF-TEST

1. You can select the entire spreadsheet by choosing the ________________ command from the ________________ menu.
2. The display format of an entry can be changed from the ________________ ____________ dialog box.
3. A ____________ switch turns a feature on or off each time you select the option.
4. The Show Values command from the Options menu is used to display ____.
5. To move the contents of a row to another row, you first place the content on the __________. You can then paste it where you want.
6. When you copy information, the original ______________, whereas if you were to move information, the original is deleted.

7. To move information from one spreadsheet to another, you would ________ or ________ the information onto the Clipboard, switch to the other spreadsheet, and ______________.
8. You can remove columns by selecting the columns and ______________ ______________________________.
9. You sort rows of information by selecting the ______________ command from the ____________ menu.
10. To sort in alphabetical order, you select ______________________ (ascending/descending) sorting order.

LESSON EIGHT

Database: Creating Files

OBJECTIVES

In this lesson you will learn how to:

- Use database terminology.
- Add a database file to the desktop.
- Specify fields to be included in the file.
- Create a numeric field.
- Enter information in a database file.
- Save a file on a disk.
- Use the concepts of list and form.
- Find information in a database.
- Print the screen display.

First, start your Macintosh and launch the Works program. Follow the instructions given in Lesson One so that the Open dialog box is displayed.

CREATING A DATABASE FILE

To create a database file, do the following:

1. Click on the Database application icon.
2. Click on the **New** button.

   The Field Name dialog box is displayed, as shown in Figure 8-1 on the following page.

At the top of the window is the database Menu Bar. In the middle of the Title Bar, the filename appears. Right now, the default filename Untitled is displayed, along with (DB) to show the part of Works you are currently using.

Figure 8-1

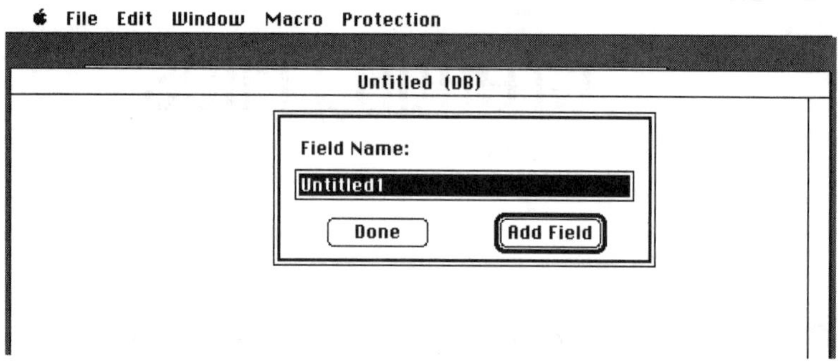

Entering Field Names

First you need to specify what information you want to keep in the file. For example, in a student file you might need to keep track of each student's identification (ID) number, name, address, telephone number, birthdate, and grade level. Each one of these items is known as a **field** in a record. Each student will then have a **record** in the database.

The field name Untitled1 already appears on the screen. If you want to use it as the name for the first field, you can. However, you will usually change it to a name that describes the contents of the first field. A field name must begin with a letter, and it cannot contain certain characters, such as asterisks, parentheses, or hyphens.

For this lesson, you are creating a file of customer records. You want to include the following fields: customer number, name, address, city, state, zip code, telephone number, credit status, and balance. Therefore, you will change Untitled1 to Cust #.

1. Type **Cust #** and click on the **Add Field** button.

   A field with the name you just typed appears in the window.

   The dialog box reappears so that you can set up another field, as shown in Figure 8-2.

Figure 8-2

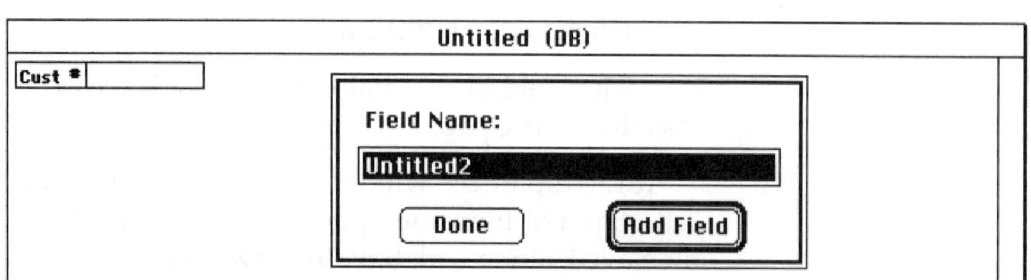

The second field is to contain the customer name. However, you will divide the customer name into two fields, First Name and Last Name.

2. Type **First Name** and click on the **Add Field** button.

   First Name appears in the window.

To enter the rest of the fields, you just type a field name, click on the Add Field button, type a field name, click on the Add Field button, and so on. Each new field appears below the previous one in the window. When you've entered all the fields, click on the Done button.

If you notice a typing error before you press a button, simply backspace and correct the error. If you notice a typing error after you press a button, don't worry about it for now. You will get a chance to correct it later.

PRACTICE TIME

Enter the rest of the fields. When you are through entering all the fields (including clicking on the Add Field button after the last entry), click on the Done button.

Last Name

Address

City

State

Zip Code

Telephone

Credit Status

Balance

All these fields were entered as text fields. That means you cannot perform calculations on any of the fields. The last field, Balance, really should be a numeric field.

Numeric Field

You might have noticed that the Menu Bar now displays more selections. The line below the Menu Bar is called the entry bar. If you have already studied the spreadsheet section, you will notice that these lines look very similar to what you saw for the spreadsheet.

1. Select the field **Balance** by pointing and clicking on it.

2. Choose **Set Field Attributes** from the **Format** menu.

   The Set Field Attributes dialog box is displayed for Balance as shown in Figure 8-3.

Figure 8-3

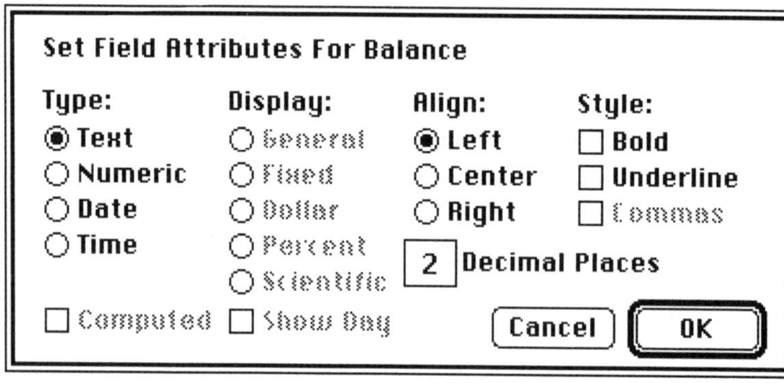

3. Click on the **Numeric** button in the first column.

   The box indicates that two decimal places would be displayed.

4. Click on the **OK** button.

Entering Records

You make an entry in a field by selecting the field and typing the data. As you type the data, it appears on the entry bar. If you notice an error, you can press Delete to back up and make corrections. When you finish typing the entry, you should visually verify the entry as displayed on the entry bar before completing the entry. Methods of completing the entry will be explained to you in just a while.

Suppose that your first customer is Sam Sherman who lives at 3983 West Blvd., Los Angeles, CA 90016. His telephone number is (213) 295-9443, and his credit rating is Preferred. His customer number is 29364, and his current balance is 356.74.

1. Select the **Cust #** field.

2. Type **29364**.

   What you type appears on the entry bar.

Notice the two check boxes on the entry bar. The box on the left that contains an X is the cancel box. The one on the right with a check in it is the enter box. You click on the enter box to complete the entry. If you decide against making the entry, you can cancel by clicking on the cancel box.

3. Click on the enter box.

   The value 29364 appears in the Cust # box.

4. Select the **First Name** field.
5. Type **Sam** and click on the enter box.

   The name Sam appears next to the First Name box.

Are you beginning to get the idea? You select the field, type your entry, then click on the enter box.

Another way to complete an entry is to press [Tab] or [Return]. When you press [Return], the entry is made, and then the field below becomes selected. When you press [Tab], the entry is made, and then the field to the right becomes selected.

PRACTICE TIME

Type entries for the rest of the fields. After you type the entry for the last field (Balance), do not press [Tab] or [Return]. Complete by clicking on the enter box so that you remain on the current form. (See Figure 8-4.)

Figure 8-4

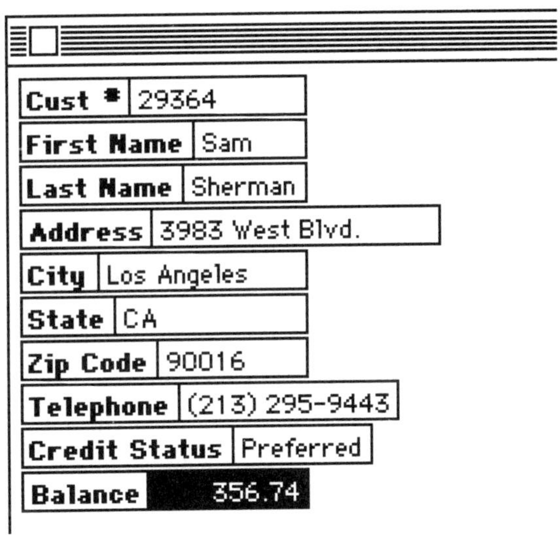

Notice on the screen that some of the field name boxes are not wide enough to display the entries. The box width only affects what is displayed, not what you enter. To make the box wider, point to the right edge of the box and drag until it is wide enough.

1. Place the pointer on the right edge of the **Address** box.

   The pointer turns into a cross.

2. Drag the mouse to the right until the box is wide enough to display its entire contents.

PRACTICE TIME

Adjust the widths of the Telephone and Credit Status boxes so that their entire entries are displayed.

When you finish filling out a record and press [Tab] or [Return], a new blank record is displayed. Right now, since you completed the entry with the enter box, you need to scroll to the next form.

Click on the down arrow on the vertical Scroll Bar at the right.

A blank entry form is displayed.

You will enter data and scroll to the next page, over and over, until you exhaust your customer data. When a blank record is displayed after you have completed the last customer record, you will press [Esc] to tell the computer you have no more records to enter. Make sure to visually check your entry for each field before pressing [Tab] or [Return].

- If you find a mistake before you press [Tab] or [Return], you can erase what you typed using [Delete] and retype.
- If you notice an error on an earlier entry, select the field and reenter the correct data.

PRACTICE TIME

Fill out nine more records using the following information. If there is no credit status indicated, leave the field blank. Stop when a blank record is displayed after you have entered the information for the last customer. Also, if you notice that the field is not wide enough to display its contents, adjust it accordingly.

Cust #:	**89238**
Name:	**Adam Martin**
Address:	**2836 Victoria Avenue**
City/State/Zip:	**Los Angeles, CA 90016**
Telephone:	**(213) 747-4221**
Credit Status:	**Good**
Balance:	**2437.18**
	19274
	Sally Davidson
	1268 Jefferson Blvd.
	Los Angeles, CA 90018
	(213) 733-4855
	Preferred
	1427.50

18392
Alex Johnson
8293 Cypress Road
Reno, NV 89503
(702) 748-9112
Good
892.00

84938
Bill Barth
9177 Honeywell Dr.
Reno, NV 89512
(702) 323-3633

400.25

97021
Jackie Swain
11836 Power Street
Sparks, NV 89431
(702) 359-4223
Preferred
3400.50

54896
Kathy Starbird
1124 Atlantic Street
Albany, CA 94706
(415) 839-4886
Good
1237.00

82394
William Peterson
3414 Indiana Ave.
San Jose, CA 95100
(408) 299-2037
Good
5060.17

47740
Larry Duncan
9051 Star Court
Downey, CA 90240
(213) 927-9727

69.00

83333
Richard Bateman
3740 San Augustin Dr.
Anaheim, CA 92800
(714) 363-4851
Good
457.25

SAVING YOUR WORK

The database file that you created is sitting on the desktop (the main memory) of the computer. If you turn off the computer, you lose that file. To keep it for future use, you must save your database file on a disk.

You will save the contents of the database on the initialized data disk. If your data disk is not initialized, the computer will prompt you when you insert the disk in the disk drive. As you recall, when you save the file, you have two choices: you can use the Save command or the Save As command.

You will use the name CUSTOMER to save the database file on the data disk.

1. Choose **Save As** from the **File** menu.

   The Save As dialog box appears, with the original name Untitled selected.

2. Type **CUSTOMER.**

   CUSTOMER replaces Untitled.

3. Make sure that the correct drive is selected for your data disk.
4. Click on the **Save** button.

Works saves the database file as a new file on the disk and changes the name on the Title Bar.

You return to the database screen.

5. Choose **Show List** from the **Format** menu. It should look like Figure 8-5.

Figure 8-5

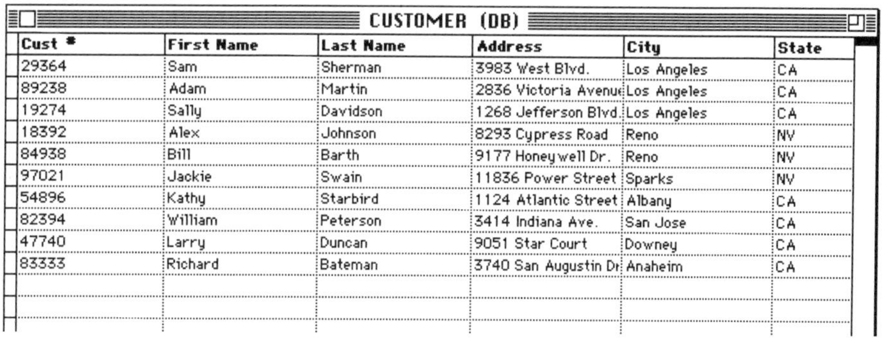

CUSTOMER (DB)

Cust #	First Name	Last Name	Address	City	State
29364	Sam	Sherman	3983 West Blvd.	Los Angeles	CA
89238	Adam	Martin	2836 Victoria Avenu	Los Angeles	CA
19274	Sally	Davidson	1268 Jefferson Blvd.	Los Angeles	CA
18392	Alex	Johnson	8293 Cypress Road	Reno	NV
84938	Bill	Barth	9177 Honeywell Dr.	Reno	NV
97021	Jackie	Swain	11836 Power Street	Sparks	NV
54896	Kathy	Starbird	1124 Atlantic Street	Albany	CA
82394	William	Peterson	3414 Indiana Ave.	San Jose	CA
47740	Larry	Duncan	9051 Star Court	Downey	CA
83333	Richard	Bateman	3740 San Augustin Dr	Anaheim	CA

THE LIST AND FORM LAYOUTS

Records (and the information) in the database can be displayed in one of two layouts: **form** or **list**. When you were entering data into records, the information was displayed using the form layout. The form layout displays records one at a time. All the fields and their contents for a single record are listed, one field per line, on the screen.

The list layout, on the other hand, displays as many as 27 records at a time. Not all fields can be displayed at any one time. Each record is displayed horizontally in one row with the appropriate information beneath the field name at the top of each column. Right now, the first six fields are displayed for all 10 records. You can see the rest of the fields by clicking on the right arrow on the horizontal Scroll Bar at the bottom.

1. Click on the right arrow on the horizontal Scroll Bar at the bottom.

   A column displaying the zip code field appears.

2. Keep on clicking on the right arrow on the horizontal Scroll Bar until you can see the Balance field.

3. Click on the left arrow on the horizontal Scroll Bar until the Customer Number (Cust #) field appears.

You can use the list layout to look through all the records in the file. Because you only have 10 records in the file, you can see the whole file on one screen. When there are more records than can be shown on one screen, you can use the vertical Scroll Bar that appears on the right edge of the screen to scroll through the other records.

CHANGING THE FIELD DISPLAY WIDTH

You might have noticed that for the fourth field, Address, the screen display is not wide enough to show the entire entry. You adjusted the field width for the form layout, but it did not affect the display width for the list layout.

You will change the width of the Address column so that it is at least as wide as the longest entry. If you find that the column is not wide enough, you can always widen it again.

1. Position the pointer on the extreme right edge of the box that displays the field name **Address**.

   The pointer turns into a cross.

2. Drag the cross to the right. When the field width is wide enough to show the longest entry in the column, release the button.

   The field width increased.

SELECTING AND PRINTING A RECORD

You can select any record by clicking on the box to the left of the row displaying the record. The selected record can then be displayed in the form layout.

1. Select Cust # 47740 by clicking to the left of the row that contains data on customer number 47740.

   The entire row is selected.

2. Choose **Show Form** from the **Format** menu.

   A form showing information on customer number 47740 is displayed.

If you would like to have a printed copy of this information, you can get one using the Print Window command from the File menu.

1. Make sure that the printer is on and is ready to use.
2. Choose **Print Window** from the **File** menu.

   The information displayed in the window is printed.
3. Choose **Show List** from the **Format** menu.

FINDING INFORMATION

Before ending this lesson, let's briefly see how information can be retrieved quickly. This is accomplished by using the Find Field command from the Organize menu.

1. With the List layout on the screen, click on the area of the screen below the data (so that nothing is selected).
2. Choose **Find Field** from the **Organize** menu.

   The Find Field dialog box is displayed, as shown in Figure 8-6.

Figure 8-6

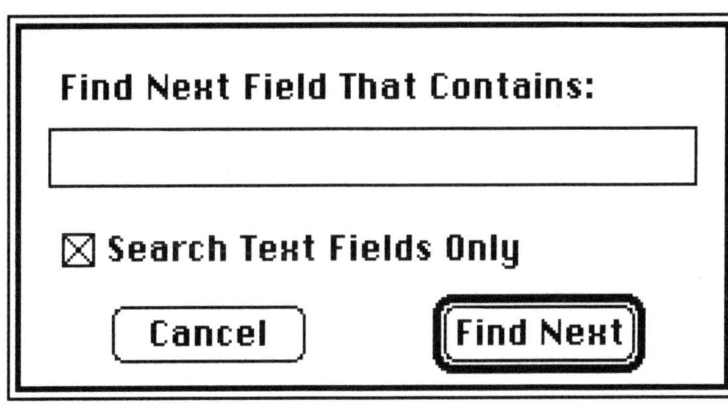

You are to specify what you want to find. Suppose you are looking for all customers whose zip code is 90016. That is, you are looking for all customer records that contain the text 90016.

3. Type **90016** and click on the **Find Next** button.

   The Zip Code column is displayed with the row containing 90016 selected.
4. Choose **Show Form** from the **Format** menu.

   The form on Sam Sherman is displayed.

5. Choose **Find Field** from the **Organize** menu again.

   90016 still appears as the field to find.

6. Click on the **Find Next** button.

   The form on Adam Martin is displayed.

7. Repeat to find the next occurrence of 90016.

   A dialog box informs you that all occurrences of 90016 have been found.

8. Click on **OK**.

You could have used the Find Field command to find a particular customer number or a particular customer name.

NOTE: The Find Field command is not case sensitive. It ignores whether the information is in uppercase or lowercase letters.

UPDATING (EDITING) THE RECORD

You might select a record to be displayed because you need to change or update information in it. Or, after looking at a record, you might find a mistake that should be corrected. In either case, you need to change (edit) the value for a field.

To change an entry, you click on the box that contains the value and retype the entry. The new entry replaces the old one. For example, suppose Sally Davidson just got married and her name is now Sally Brown. You will have to update her record.

1. Choose **Show List** from the **Format** menu.
2. Click on the box that contains the last name Davidson.
3. Type **Brown** and complete the entry.

This is the end of this lesson. Quit Works following the procedure described in Lesson One. Make sure to save the changes.

■ SUMMARY

Topic or Feature	*Command or Reference*	*Menu*	*Page*
Enter Field Names	Type field name Click on Add Field		84

Topic or Feature	*Command or Reference*	*Menu*	*Page*
Specify a Field as Numeric	Set Field Attributes	Format	85
Complete an Entry	Click on the enter box or press [Tab] or [Return]		86
Adjust the Width of Field Boxes in the Form Layout	Position pointer on the right edge of the box and drag		87
Save a File	Save or Save As	File	90
Display in Form Layout	Show Form	Format	91
Display in List Layout	Show List	Format	91
Change Field Width in the List Layout	Position pointer on the line between columns and drag		92
Print a Form	Print Window	File	92
Find a Record	Find Field	Organize	93

■ *SELF-TEST*

1. In an inventory database, a record might be composed of the following ________________: purchase date, item description, location, and value.
2. To specify a field as a numeric field, you select the field then choose the ________________ command from the ________________ menu.
3. A cancel box is used to ________________________________.
4. When you complete an entry by pressing ________________, the entry is made, then the field below becomes selected.
5. A field name box on a form can be widened by ______________________ ____ ____.
6. On a ______________ layout, each record appears horizontally in one row with the appropriate information beneath the field names at the top of each column.
7. To change the field display width, you position the pointer on the line between columns and drag. The cursor should turn into a ____________.
8. To change the content of a field, you select the field and ______________.

9. To get a printout of a form, choose the ________________ command from the ________________ menu.
10. To find a record containing certain text, choose the ________________ command from the ________________ menu.

LESSON NINE

Database: Manipulating the Data

OBJECTIVES

In this lesson you will learn how to:

- Arrange (sort) records in a database file.
- Select records based on single, multiple, and numeric specifications.
- Update (change) information in existing records.
- Change the display format of multiple-records layout.
- Insert records in an existing database file.
- Copy records within a database file.
- Delete records in a database file.
- Save a database file to disk using the same filename.

Start your Macintosh and launch the Works program so that the Open dialog box is displayed. Make sure that you have the data disk from Lesson Eight in the drive.

First you will retrieve the database file from the last lesson.

1. Click on the Database application icon.
2. Make sure that the drive for your data disk has been selected.
3. Select the file CUSTOMER on the list box, and click on the **Open** button. Change the format to list.

   The database from the previous lesson is displayed on the screen.

PRACTICE TIME

Display the form for customer number 82394, William Peterson. Do not use the Find Field command.

How did you do? Although this file does not contain very many records, it still took you a while to find customer number 82394 in the list format, didn't it? This is because the records are not in any specific order. What if there were 1,000 records? If the display was organized by customer number, it would not be as difficult.

ARRANGING RECORDS

Works allows you to rearrange the records in a file in whatever order you want. Records can be arranged in alphabetical order (A to Z or Z to A) or in numerical order (ascending or descending) for any category you select.

Let's rearrange the CUSTOMER file so that the records are in ascending numerical order by customer number. This is done using the Sort command.

1. Click anywhere in the first column of the list layout (where customer number is displayed).
2. Choose **Sort** from the **Organize** menu.

   The dialog box as shown in Figure 9-1 is displayed.

Figure 9-1

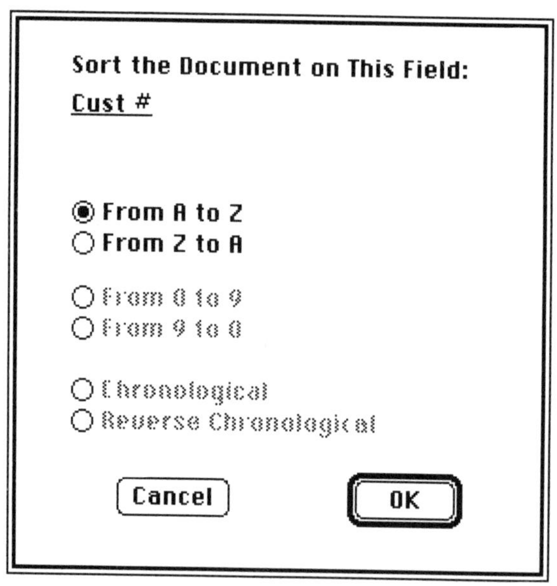

The box shows that you've specified the file to be sorted on customer number field. The default is to sort in alphabetical order (A to Z). Although the customer number field contains numbers, it is a text field and hence sorting in alphabetical order will put it in ascending numerical sequence.

3. Click on the **OK** button.

   The list layout is displayed, and the records are now rearranged as shown in Figure 9-2.

Figure 9-2

CUSTOMER (DB)

Cust #	First Name	Last Name	Address	City	State
18392	Alex	Johnson	8293 Cypress Road	Reno	NV
19274	Sally	Brown	1268 Jefferson Blvd.	Los Angeles	CA
29364	Sam	Sherman	3983 West Blvd.	Los Angeles	CA
47740	Larry	Duncan	9051 Star Court	Downey	CA
54896	Kathy	Starbird	1124 Atlantic Street	Albany	CA
82394	William	Peterson	3414 Indiana Ave.	San Jose	CA
83333	Richard	Bateman	3740 San Augustin Dr.	Anaheim	CA
84938	Bill	Barth	9177 Honeywell Dr.	Reno	NV
89238	Adam	Martin	2836 Victoria Avenue	Los Angeles	CA
97021	Jackie	Swain	11836 Power Street	Sparks	NV

That was fast, wasn't it? Let's now rearrange the file in alphabetical order by last names.

1. Click on the **Last Name** column (third column).
2. Choose **Sort** from the **Organize** menu.
3. Click on the **OK** button.

   The records are now arranged in alphabetical order by last name.

You can use the Sort command from the form layout as well. All you have to do is select the field on which you want to sort and choose the Sort command.

PRACTICE TIME

Put the records back in ascending numerical order by customer number.

RECORD SELECTION

The Find Field command is very useful for locating those records that contain a certain value (or entry). However, you cannot specify which field to search for that value. For example, suppose that you are looking for a record that contains the text "star." Works will locate both the record for Kathy Starbird and the one for Larry Duncan who lives on Star Court.

You can be more specific using the Record Selection command from the Organize menu.

1. Choose **Record Selection** from the **Organize** menu.

   The Record Selection window as shown in Figure 9-3 is displayed.

Figure 9-3

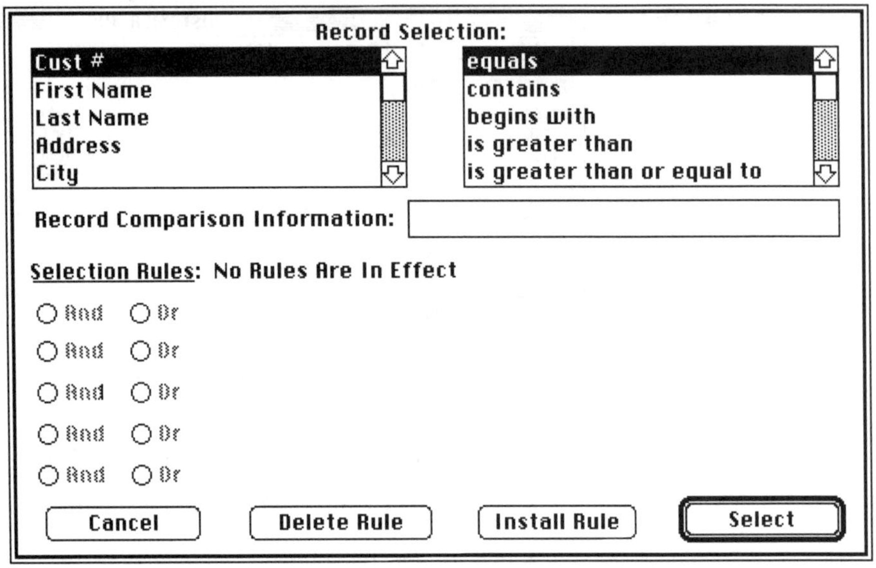

You are to specify what field you want to use as the basis of selection. Let's select all customers whose telephone area code is 702. The field for selection, then, is Telephone. The scroll box on the left displays all field names.

2. Select **Telephone** in the field name scroll box.

Now you need to specify whether you are looking for a specific telephone number, a telephone number whose value is greater or less than a specified value, a telephone number that begins with specified characters, and so on. You are looking for customers whose telephone number begins with the area code (702). The conditions you can specify are displayed in the scroll box on the right.

3. Select **begins with** in the condition scroll box on the right.

Now you need to specify the text the desired telephone number is to begin with.

4. Type **(702)**, then click on the **Install Rule** button at the bottom.

   Selection Rule is set to **Telephone begins with (702)**.

5. Now click on the **Select** button.

   The list screen is displayed showing only those records that meet the selection criteria, as shown in Figure 9-4.

6. To list all records again, choose **Show All Records** from the **Organize** menu.

Figure 9-4

CUSTOMER (DB)

Cust #	First Name	Last Name	Address	City	State
18392	Alex	Johnson	8293 Cypress Road	Reno	NV
84938	Bill	Barth	9177 Honeywell Dr.	Reno	NV
97021	Jackie	Swain	11836 Power Street	Sparks	NV

PRACTICE TIME

Specify the selection rules so that only the records meeting the following are displayed. Before specifying each rule, however, click on the Delete Rule button to erase the previous selection rule.

1. The customer number contains the digit 3 anywhere within it.
2. The Credit Status category contains a value (is not blank).
3. Display all records again.

MULTIPLE SELECTION RULE

You can use more than one rule for record selection. For example, you can look for customers who live in Nevada (NV) and have Good credit status.

1. Choose **Record Selection** from the **Organize** menu.
2. Click the **Delete Rule** button to clear the previously specified rule.

When you have two selection criteria, you enter them one at a time, with a connector in between them. First, you will enter the selection criteria for the state. You want the content of State to equal NV.

3. Select **STATE** from the field scroll box.
4. Select **equals** from the condition scroll box.
5. Type NV and click on the **Install Rule** button.

   The selection rule reads State equals NV.

Now you need to enter the connector. Your options are "And" and "Or." The default is set to Or.

And	Records must meet **both** the selection rule that you've already entered and the one you will enter next.
Or	Records must meet **either** the selection rule that you've already entered or the one you will enter next.

6. Click on the first **And** button.
7. Select **Credit Status** from the field name scroll box.
8. Select **equals** from the condition scroll box.
9. Type **Good** and click on the **Install Rule** button.

   The selection rule now reads State equals NV and Credit Status equals Good.
10. Click on the **Select** button.

    Alex Johnson is the only record that meets the criteria.
11. Display all records again.

NUMERIC RANGE SELECTION

Sometimes you need to select records that contain values within a certain numeric range, such as to find all the customers whose balance is between $1,000 and $2,000.

1. Choose **Record Selection** from the **Organize** menu.
2. Click on the **Delete Rule** button twice to erase previously set rules.
3. Select **Balance** from the field name scroll box.
4. Select **is greater than or equal to** from the condition scroll box.
5. Type **1000** and click on the **Install Rule** button.
6. Click on the first **And** button.
7. Select **Balance** from the field name scroll box.
8. Select **is less than or equal to** from the condition scroll box.
9. Type **2000** and click on the **Install Rule** button.
10. Click on the **Select** button.

    Two records meeting the selection rules are displayed.
11. Display all records again.

PRACTICE TIME

Try changing the record selection rules.

1. Select all customers whose zip code is in the range 90000 to 90050.
2. Select all customers whose last names do not contain the character A.
3. Select all customers whose zip code is not within the range 90000 to 99999.
4. Display all records again.

CHANGING FIELD DISPLAY ORDER

You can change the order in which fields appear in the list layout. Because the first five fields are displayed, changing the order changes which fields are displayed together.

Suppose that you decide that it would be more useful if the credit status and balance were displayed next to the customer name. That is, you want to move Credit Status and Balance (which are the last two fields on the record) to the fourth and fifth positions, respectively.

1. Make sure that you are using the list layout.
2. Scroll the screen until the Credit Status field is displayed.
3. Position the pointer on the field name **Credit Status**.

   The pointer turns into a hand.
4. Drag the hand to the left. As you do, various field names change color. Also, the screen scrolls to reveal fields to the left. When the hand is on the **Address** field, release the mouse button.

   The Credit Status field now appears to the left of the Address field.

NOTE: When the field is dragged to the left, it will be placed to the left of the field that the hand is on. When it is dragged to the right, it will be placed to the right of the field that the hand is on.

5. Choose **Show Form** from the **Format** menu.

   The Credit Status field still appears after the Telephone field.

NOTE: Changing the display order in the list layout does not change the order in which fields are stored in the database file.

PRACTICE TIME

1. Move the Balance field column so that it is the fifth field in the records, right after Credit Status.
2. Move the Credit Status and Balance fields back to where they were before—the last two fields in the record.

INSERTING A RECORD

You just got a new customer. He is to be customer number 69248. His name is Bruce Morrison, and he lives at 2080 Guatemala Street, Beaverton, OR 97005. His telephone number is (503) 646-6892. He does not have a credit status yet, and his balance is $125.00. You would like to insert his record in the file so that the file is still in ascending numerical order by customer number. This can be done by adding a record to the end of the file and sorting the file again by customer number.

But right now, you will insert the record at its proper place in sequence from the list layout.

1. Make sure that you are in list layout and that the records are in ascending numerical order by customer number.

Customer number 69248 should go between customer numbers 54896 and 82394. New records are always inserted immediately before the record that is selected. In this case, you want to select the record of customer number 82394.

2. Select the record for customer number 82394 by clicking to the left of the row.
3. Choose **Insert Record** from the **Edit** menu.

   A blank row opens up between customer numbers 54896 and 82394.
4. Choose **Show Form** from the **Format** menu.

   A blank form is displayed.
5. Enter the information for all fields.

   After you press the final Return, the form for customer number 82394 is displayed.
6. Choose **Show List** from the **Format** menu.

NOTE: You can insert a record from the form layout as well. When you issue the Insert Record command, the record is inserted immediately before the record that was displayed.

COPY RECORDS

In creating (inserting) new records, if some of the new entries are the same as in an existing record, you can copy these. You can copy an entire record or just some fields.

William Peterson's wife, Joan, is a new customer. You will copy last name, address, and telephone number from William Peterson's record. The new customer number is 32097. Her balance is 247.09 and she does not have a credit status yet. Also, this time, you will add this information to the end of the record and resort on customer number.

William Peterson's customer number is 82394.

1. Select **Last Name**, **Address**, **City**, **State**, **Zip Code**, and **Telephone** fields from William Peterson's record. This is done by pointing to the **Last Name** field and pressing and holding down the mouse button as you drag the mouse to the right, until all these fields are selected. You can then release the mouse button. The result is shown in Figure 9-5.

Figure 9-5

CUSTOMER (DB)

Cust #	First Name	Last Name	Address	City	State
18392	Alex	Johnson	8293 Cypress Road	Reno	NV
19274	Sally	Brown	1268 Jefferson Blvd.	Los Angeles	CA
29364	Sam	Sherman	3983 West Blvd.	Los Angeles	CA
47740	Larry	Duncan	9051 Star Court	Downey	CA
54896	Kathy	Starbird	1124 Atlantic Street	Albany	CA
69248	Bruce	Morrison	2080 Guatemala Street	Beaverton	OR
82394	William	Peterson	3414 Indiana Ave.	San Jose	CA
83333	Richard	Bateman	3740 San Augustin Dr.	Anaheim	CA
84938	Bill	Barth	9177 Honeywell Dr.	Reno	NV
89238	Adam	Martin	2836 Victoria Ave.	Los Angeles	CA
97021	Jackie	Swain	11836 Power Street	Sparks	NV

2. Choose **Copy** from the **Edit** menu.

   The information is placed on the Clipboard.

3. Click on the blank space below the last record, in the **Last Name** field (on the box below Swain).

4. Choose **Paste** from the **Edit** menu.

   The information is placed on the specified row.

5. Choose **Show Form** from the **Format** menu.

   Now you need to fill in the rest of the information.

PRACTICE TIME

1. Fill in the rest of the information: the customer number is 32097 and the first name is Joan. Also, the credit status is left blank and the balance is 247.09.
2. Sort the records in ascending order by customer number.

DELETING A RECORD

Now that you know how to insert a record, let's delete a record. You will delete the record for Richard Bateman. Again, this can be done from either the list or the form layout. The command will delete the record that is selected.

1. Make sure that you are in the list layout.
2. Select Richard Bateman's record. His customer number is 83333.
3. Choose **Cut** from the **Edit** menu.

   Richard Bateman's record is deleted. (Actually, the record was not completely deleted. It has been placed on the Clipboard.)
4. Choose **Show Clipboard** from the **Window** menu.

   The content of the Clipboard is displayed as shown in Figure 9-6.

Figure 9-6

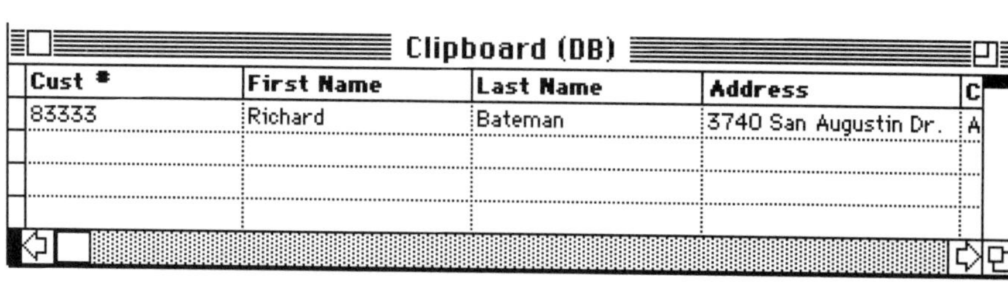

5. Close the Clipboard window.

If you had deleted the record by mistake, you could still retrieve it from the Clipboard by using the Paste command from the Edit menu.

You can delete consecutive records by selecting the records and issuing the Cut command. If you want to delete multiple records that meet specific criteria (but are not necessarily consecutive records in the file), use the Record Selection command, so that only the selected records are displayed on the screen. You can then cut all of them at once. You may try this feature on your own.

QUICK SAVE

You have made quite a few changes to the CUSTOMER file. These changes were made only to the version that is on the desktop. The file that is on the disk has not been changed at all. If you turn the computer off or if there is a power failure, all the changes you made in this lesson will be lost.

PRACTICE TIME

Save the file as CUSTOMER 1.

This is the end of this lesson. Quit Works as described in Lesson One.

■ *SUMMARY*

Topic or Feature	*Command or Reference*	*Menu*	*Page*
Arrange Records	Sort	Organize	98
Record Selection	Record Selection	Organize	99
Multiple Selection Rule	Multiple selection criteria are specified using connectors		101
Change Field Display Order	Place pointer on the field name and drag		103
Insert a Record	Insert Record	Edit	104
Copy Record	Select fields to copy		105
	Copy	Edit	
	Select position to copy to		
	Paste	Edit	
Delete a Record	Cut	Edit	106

■ SELF-TEST

1. To arrange the database file in order by a specific field, you __________, then choose the Sort command from the Organize menu.
2. Changes made to the form layout __________ (do/do not) affect the list layout.
3. To specify the selection rule, you choose the __________ command from the __________ menu.
4. In setting multiple selection rules, the connector __________ (And/Or) means that both conditions must be met.
5. The selection rule for all customers whose balance is between $100 and $200, might read as follows: ____________________ ____________________.
6. To change the display order in the list layout, you click on the __________ __________ and drag the field to where you want it to appear.
7. When you position the pointer on a field name, the pointer turns into a __________.
8. When you insert a new record into the middle of a database file, it is inserted __________ the record selected.
9. To copy information from one record to another, you place it on the __________.
10. To delete a record from the database file, you choose the __________ command from the __________ menu.

LESSON TEN

Database: Printing a Report and Changing Structure

OBJECTIVES

In this lesson you will learn how to:

- Understand the concept of report format.
- Define a report format.
- Define a report format with selected records.
- Define a report format with selected fields.
- Change the database structure.

Start your Macintosh and launch the Works program so that the Open dialog box is displayed. Make sure that you have the data disk from Lesson Nine in the drive.

First you will retrieve the database file from the last lesson.

1. Click on the Database application icon.
2. Make sure that the drive for your data disk has been selected.
3. Select the file CUSTOMER 1 on the list box, and click on the **Open** button. Change the format to list.

   The database from the previous lesson is displayed on the screen.

DEFINING A REPORT

To print information from the database, you print a report. You specify the contents and format of a report by setting up a report definition. Here, you will create a customer listing. First, you will create a report listing all fields for all customers.

Before defining the report, you will adjust the column widths of the list layout to eliminate any unnecessary spaces. This is not a required step; you are just doing it so you won't have to adjust the column width within each report definition.

1. Adjust the widths of all columns to eliminate any unnecessary spaces.

2. Choose **New Report** from the **Report** menu.

   A screen similar to Figure 10-1 is displayed. (Your screen may look different because the widths of your fields may be different from those shown here.)

Figure 10-1

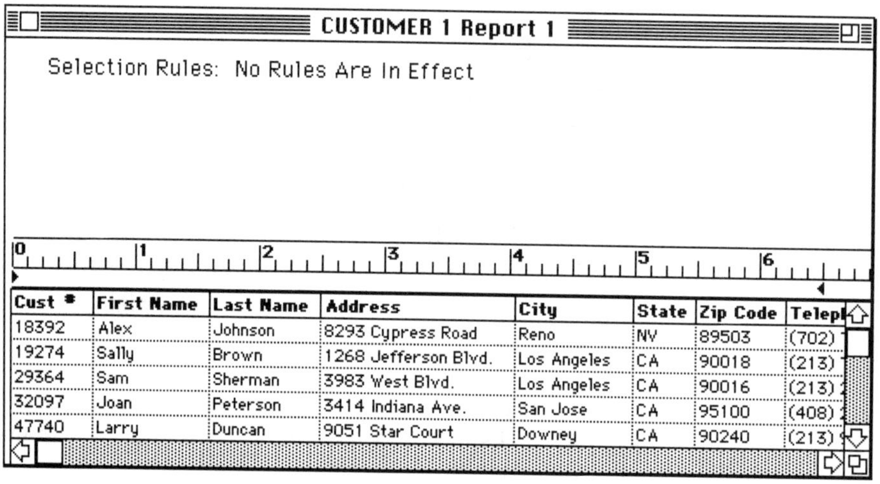

At the top of the window is the title CUSTOMER 1 Report 1. Works has automatically assigned a default name of Report 1 to your report definition. Let's change it to something that makes a little more sense.

3. Choose **Change Report Title** from the **Edit** menu.

   The Report Title dialog box is displayed as shown in Figure 10-2.

Figure 10-2

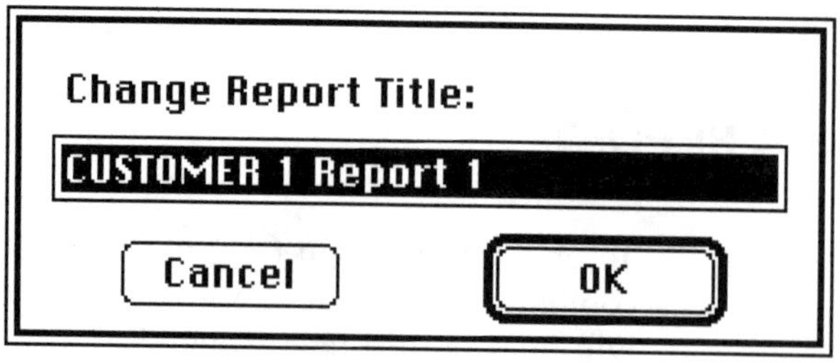

4. Type **Customer Listing** and click on the **OK** button.

In the middle of the window is a Ruler Line similar to the one in the word processor. It shows the left-edge marker ▸ at 0 inches and the right-edge marker ◂ at 6½ inches. Works will print any part of the database that appears between these two markers. It assumes you are using 8½-inch-wide paper with 1-inch margins on both sides.

5. Scroll the database display to the right, to display the **Balance** field, as shown in Figure 10-3.

Figure 10-3

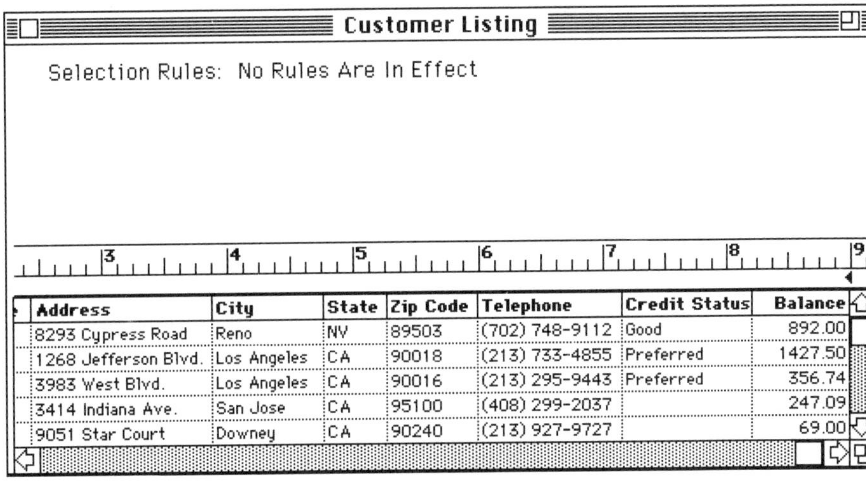

You will notice that the database is about 9 inches wide. This would fit on a paper that is 11 inches wide, with 1-inch margins on either edge—that is, horizontally on a standard 8½″ by 11″ paper.

NOTE: If your database does not fit within 9 inches, you will need to adjust some column widths until it does. This adjustment can be made on the database display in this window. Any change made here, however, only affects the report printed. The changes will not affect the list layout of the database.

If, for some reason, you cannot reduce the width to 9 inches, then you will have to reduce the left and right margin settings. The default is 1 inch. The paper is 11 inches wide. Subtract the width of your database from 11 inches, then divide the remainder by two. The result is the margin settings. Press [Tab] *until the left margin box is highlighted and enter the number. Then press* [Tab] *and enter the right margin. (With this database, the width should never be more than 10 inches.)*

6. Choose **Page Setup** from the **File** menu.

   The Page Setup dialog box is displayed.

7. Click on the horizontal orientation icon, as displayed in Figures 10-4(a) and 10-4(b).

You will now enter a title for the report. The title is entered in the Header box. The following formatting commands are available.

Figure 10-4(a)

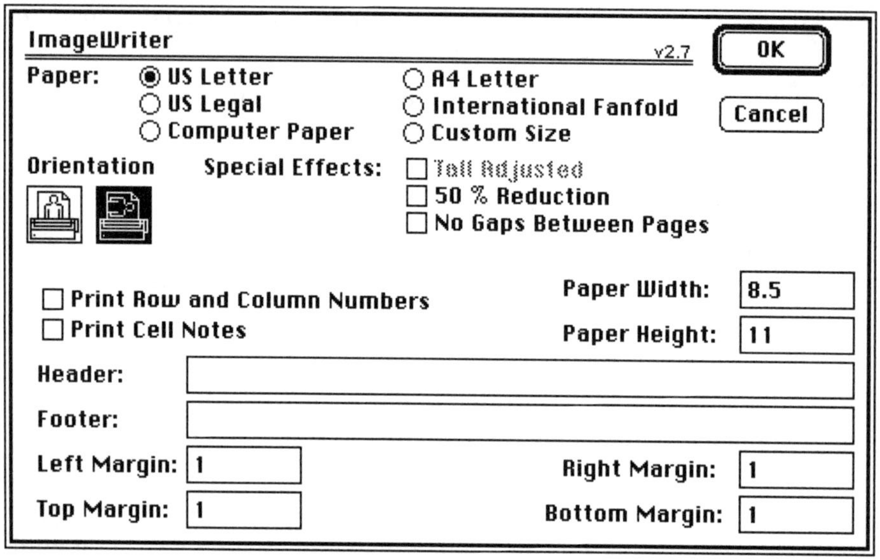

Figure 10-4(b)

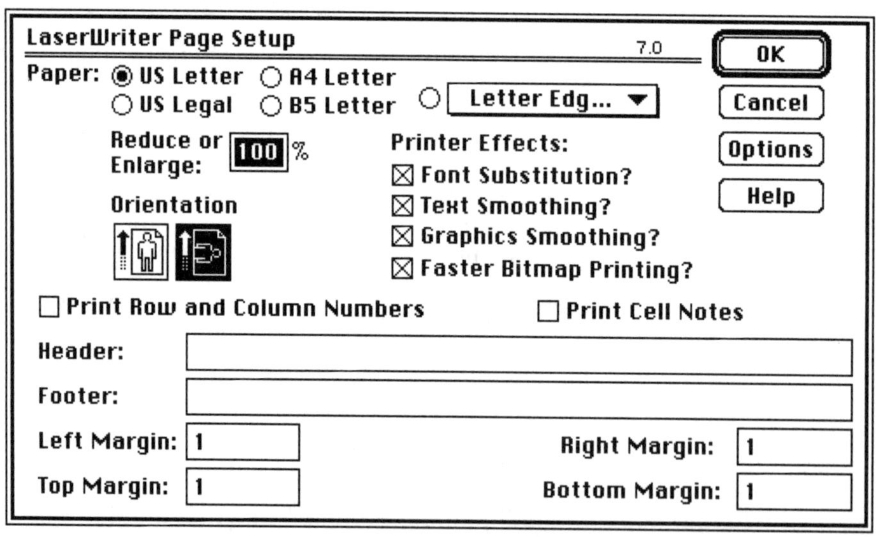

&l Align the following characters at the left margin.

&c Center the following characters.

&r Align the following characters at the right margin.

&d Print the current date.

&p Print the page number.

&b Print the following characters in bold.

You will call this report Customer Listing; you want the title centered and in bold characters.

8. Press [Tab] until the insertion bar appears in the Header.
9. Type **&c&bCustomer Listing** and click on the **OK** button.

Now you are ready to print the report. Before you actually print a report, however, you will preview it on the screen.

10. Choose **Print** from the **File** menu.

    The Print dialog box similar to the ones shown in Figures 10-5(a) and 10-5(b) is displayed.

Figure 10-5(a)

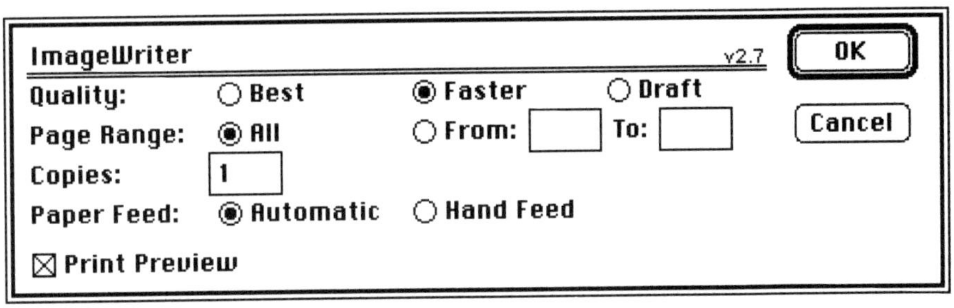

Figure 10-5(b)

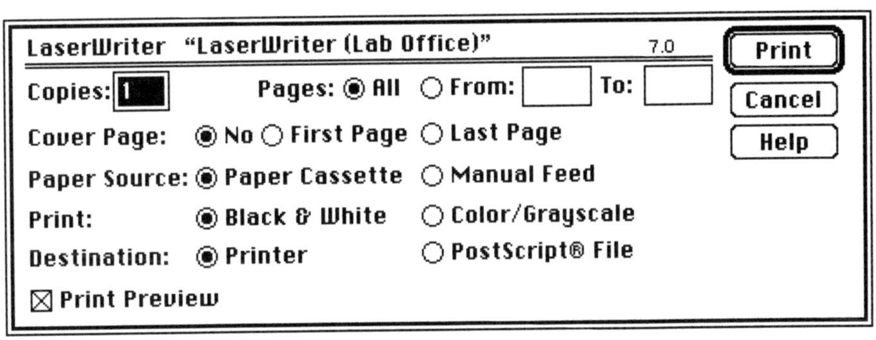

At the bottom left corner is a box for Print Preview.

11. Click on the **Print Preview** box.

    An X appears in the box.

12. Click on the **OK** or **Print** button.

    The preview screen as shown in Figure 10-6 is displayed.

Although it may be difficult to make out individual words, the preview screen gives a good idea of what the end result will look like.

13. If you are satisfied with the preview of the report, click on the **Print** button. If not, click on the **Cancel** button. You can go back and modify the report.

Figure 10-6

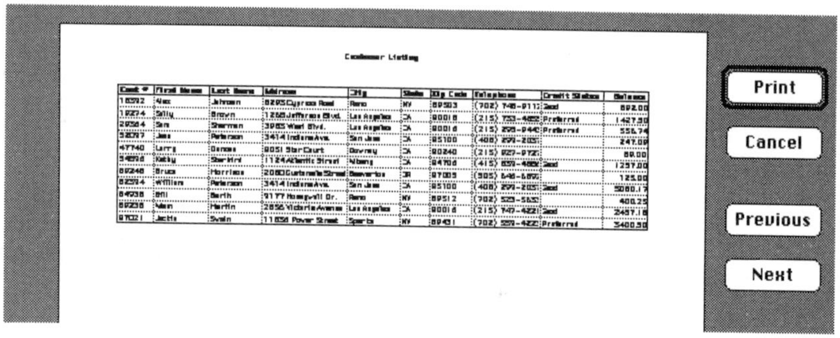

SAVING A REPORT

When you close the report definition window, the report becomes a part of the database.

1. Close the report definition screen.
2. Choose **Select Report** from the **Report** menu.

   You will notice that Customer Listing is listed.
3. Click on the **Cancel** button.

Although this report definition is part of the database, it is not saved on the disk until you save the database CUSTOMER 1 on the disk.

A REPORT CONTAINING SELECTED RECORDS

You will now define format for a report that contains just the selected records. Since the report format is just about the same as the one already created, you will duplicate it.

1. Choose **Duplicate Report** from the **Report** menu.

   The Duplicate Report dialog box is displayed, as shown in Figure 10-7.
2. Select **Customer Listing** and click on the **OK** button.

PRACTICE TIME

1. Change the report title to **Customer Listing for Nevada.**
2. Change the header to **Customer Listing for Nevada.**

Figure 10-7

Record selection is specified through the Record Selection command in the Organize menu. You are already familiar with this command.

3. Choose **Record Selection** from the **Organize** menu.

   The Record Selection dialog box is displayed.

4. Make sure that any previously specified selection rules are deleted.
5. Install the selection rule for all customers who live in Nevada (State equals NV).
6. Click on the **Select** button.

   You will notice that only three customers are displayed.

PRACTICE TIME

1. Preview and print the report.
2. Close the report definition.

A REPORT CONTAINING SELECTED FIELDS

Let's say that you want a report that shows just the customer's last name, first name, and balance. To do this, you move those fields you want displayed within the print area (the area between the two edge markers) and move the rest of the fields out. You learned how to move fields in Lesson Nine.

1. Start a new report.
2. In the database report display in the window, move the Last Name field to the left of the Cust # field.
3. Move the First Name and Balance fields next to the Last Name field.

The idea is to move the rest of the fields to the right of the right-edge marker. This can be done by moving the right-edge marker, by increasing the width of the three fields you want printed, or by printing the report in larger type size. You will do all three. At any time, if you wonder what the final product will look like, you can preview the report.

4. Choose **Size** from the **Format** menu but *do not release the mouse button.*

   Another menu is displayed as shown in Figure 10-8.

5. Without releasing the mouse button, highlight **14 Point**, then release the button.

   The characters on the screen are much larger. (Initially, there was a check mark in front of 9 points. You increased the size of the characters from 9 points to 14 points.)

6. Increase the column widths of the Last Name, First Name, and Balance fields. Make sure that the right edge of the Balance column is still within the print area.
7. If necessary, move the right-edge marker (by pointing and dragging) to the right edge of the Balance field.

Figure 10-8

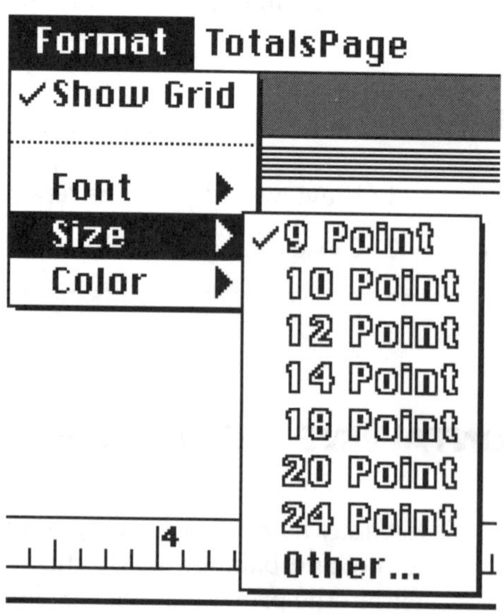

8. Preview the report.

If you want your report centered on the page, you will have to figure out the new margin settings. If, for example, your right-edge marker is on 4½ inches on the Ruler Line, you subtract that from 8½ inches (the width of the paper). That leaves 4 inches. Divide that by two. That means you need to set both the left and right margins to 2 inches.

9. Calculate margin settings.
10. From the Page Setup dialog box, specify the proper margins. Also, set the header to **&c&bBalances**.
11. Change the report title to **Balances**.
12. Preview and print the report.

If you want customer names listed in alphabetical order by the last name, you have to sort the database outside the report screen. Sorting has to be done on the entire database. It cannot be done in the report screen.

1. Close the report screen.
2. Click anywhere on the **Last Name** column.
3. Choose **Sort** from the **Organize** menu.
4. Sort from A to Z.
5. Choose **Select Report** from the **Report** menu.
6. Select **Balances**.

DISPLAYING TOTAL

If you recall, the Balance field was defined as a numeric field. When a field is defined as numeric, you can have the numbers totaled in a report.

1. Select the **Balance** field by clicking on the field name.
2. Choose **Sum This Field** from the **TotalPage** menu.
3. Preview the report.

   The total for the Balance field is printed as shown in Figure 10-9.
4. Close the report screen.
5. Close the database so that all report definitions are saved along with the database.

Figure 10-9

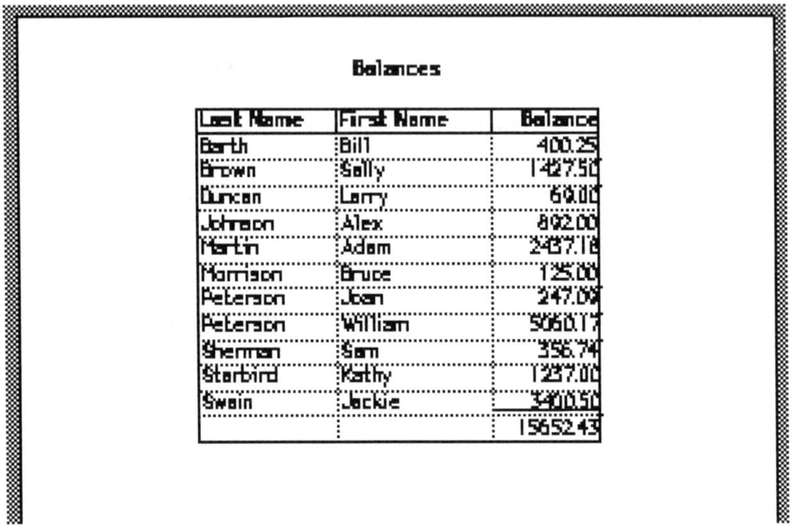

Balances

Last Name	First Name	Balance
Barth	Bill	400.25
Brown	Sally	1427.50
Duncan	Larry	69.00
Johnson	Alex	892.00
Martin	Adam	2437.18
Morrison	Bruce	125.00
Peterson	Joan	247.09
Peterson	William	5060.17
Sherman	Sam	356.74
Starbird	Kathy	1237.00
Swain	Jackie	3400.50
		15652.43

NOTE: Any changes made to the database from within the report definition screen are internal to the screen definition. These changes did not affect the actual database. You only specified what the printed report is to look like.

CHANGING DATABASE STRUCTURE

Insert a Field

While you are looking over your reports and patting yourself on the back for a job well done, all of a sudden it occurs to you that you forgot to include a field. The report needs to include a field named Region because there is a different sales representative for each region. The Pacific Northwest is Region 1, Northern California is Region 2, Southern California is Region 3, and Nevada is Region 5.

Does this mean you have to start all over again and create a new database? The answer is no.

1. Open CUSTOMER 1.
2. Choose **Add New Field** from the **Edit** menu.

   A dialog box appears asking you for the field name.
3. Type **Region** and click on the **Add Field** button.

   The field Region is added at the end of the database.

PRACTICE TIME

1. For each record, enter the appropriate value for the Region field.

   Pacific Northwest is Region 1.

   Northern California is Region 2.

   Southern California is Region 3.

   Nevada is Region 5.

   Hints: The state of Oregon is in the Pacific Northwest. The cities of San Jose and Albany are in Northern California. The cities of Downey and Los Angeles are in Southern California.

2. Save the database as CUSTOMER 2.
3. Select and display the customers in Region 3.

Delete a Field

The change you want to make to the database structure might be to delete a field. You will now delete the newly inserted Region field for practice.

1. Select the **Region** field by clicking on the field name.
2. Choose **Delete Field** from the **Edit** menu.

   The field has been deleted.

This is the end of this lesson. Quit Works as described in Lesson One. There is no need to save the changes.

■ *SUMMARY*

Topic or Feature	*Command or Reference*	*Menu*	*Page*
Define a New Report	New Report	Report	109
Change Report Title	Change Report Title	Edit	110
Copy the Definition of an Existing Report	Duplicate Report	Report	114
Report Displaying Selected Records	Record Selection	Organize	114
Report Displaying Selected Fields	Move fields to display between the two edge markers		115

Topic or Feature	*Command or Reference*	*Menu*	*Page*
Change Print Size	Size	Format	116
Display Total	Sum This Field	TotalPage	117
Add New Fields	Add New Field	Edit	118
Delete Fields	Delete Field	Edit	119

■ SELF-TEST

1. To change the title of the report, you choose the ______________ command from the ______________ menu.
2. A report is attached to the database for which it's defined. It is saved when you save the ____________________.
3. In order for a field to appear in a report, it must be located between the two __________________.
4. To print a report with a heading (title), the text for the heading must be specified as ______________.
5. If you want the heading STUDENT ROSTER to appear centered and in bold characters, you enter it in the header preceded with ____________.
6. To display selected records in a report, you specify the ______________ rule through the ______________ command in the ______________ menu.
7. In specifying the character size, 9-point characters are ______________ (smaller/larger) than 14-point characters.
8. If you are using a standard 8½-inch-wide paper and the width of the print area is 3½ inches, you need to set margins to ______________ inches to have the report centered.
9. To print the total for an amount field, you select the field then choose the ______________ command from the ______________ menu.
10. When you add a field to a database, all existing fields ______________ (are deleted/remain intact).

LESSON ELEVEN

Moving Information Between Applications

OBJECTIVES

In this lesson you will learn how to:

- Transfer information between the word processor, spreadsheet, and database applications.
- Use the merge feature.

Start your Macintosh and launch the Works program so that the Open dialog box is displayed. Make sure that you have a data disk.

Before starting this lesson, make sure that you know how to use the word-processing, spreadsheet, and database applications of Microsoft Works. This lesson explains the steps involved in transferring files. The examples used are not necessarily true-to-life situations.

MOVING INFORMATION FROM SPREADSHEET TO WORD PROCESSOR

First you will create a spreadsheet file to be used for data transfer purposes. Then you will write a document to be used to receive information from a spreadsheet.

1. Create the following spreadsheet file:

	A	B	C	D	E	F
1			SALARY DATA			
2						
3	NAME	NAME			NUM	
4	LAST	FIRST	SEX	DEPT	YEARS	SALARY
5	Barth	Bill	M	Mkt	25	45000
6	Billings	Sandy	F	Acct	30	32000
7	Cole	Ron	M	Sales	10	28000
8	Cotman	Sharon	F	Acct	7	49000
9	Harry	Daria	F	Sales	26	38000
10	Hart	Ed	M	Mkt	4	52000
11	Holloway	Cathy	F	Mkt	7	43595

12	Humphreys	Pat	F	Acct	15	23450
13	Manske	Ken	M	Sales	17	30400
14	McNerney	Charles	M	Mkt	8	42900
15	Myers	Bill	M	Sales	13	37400
16	Nau	Bob	M	Mkt	7	43595
17	Sachs	Arline	F	Mkt	8	42900
18	Thomas	Margaret	F	Sales	11	47000
19	Wiggs	Laura	F	Acct	23	52700
20	Wilkinson	Stan	M	Sales	20	63000

2. Adjust column width, change the display format for the row headings, and change the font as appropriate.
3. Save the spreadsheet as SP CHAP 11 on your data disk.

   Your spreadsheet should be similar to the one shown in Figure 11-1.

Figure 11-1

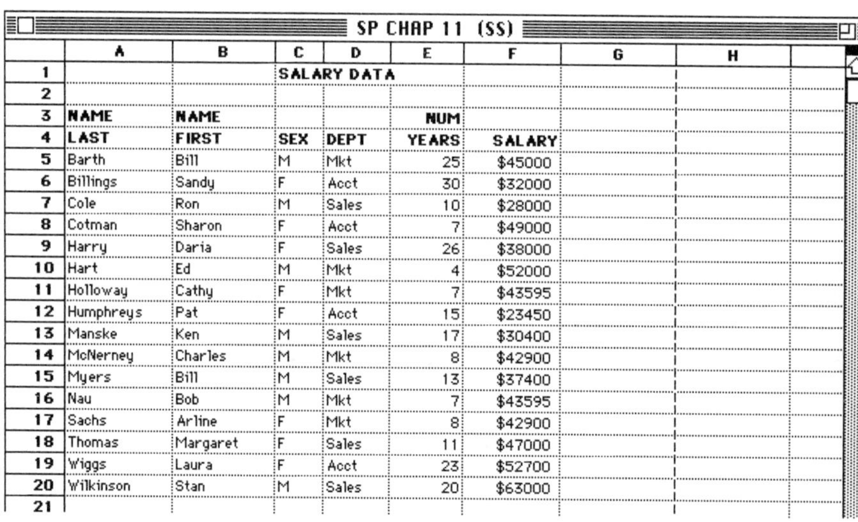

SP CHAP 11 (SS)

	A	B	C	D	E	F	G	H
1			SALARY DATA					
2								
3	NAME	NAME			NUM			
4	LAST	FIRST	SEX	DEPT	YEARS	SALARY		
5	Barth	Bill	M	Mkt	25	$45000		
6	Billings	Sandy	F	Acct	30	$32000		
7	Cole	Ron	M	Sales	10	$28000		
8	Cotman	Sharon	F	Acct	7	$49000		
9	Harry	Daria	F	Sales	26	$38000		
10	Hart	Ed	M	Mkt	4	$52000		
11	Holloway	Cathy	F	Mkt	7	$43595		
12	Humphreys	Pat	F	Acct	15	$23450		
13	Manske	Ken	M	Sales	17	$30400		
14	McNerney	Charles	M	Mkt	8	$42900		
15	Myers	Bill	M	Sales	13	$37400		
16	Nau	Bob	M	Mkt	7	$43595		
17	Sachs	Arline	F	Mkt	8	$42900		
18	Thomas	Margaret	F	Sales	11	$47000		
19	Wiggs	Laura	F	Acct	23	$52700		
20	Wilkinson	Stan	M	Sales	20	$63000		
21								

4. Create a new word processor file and enter the following document, which is incomplete:

   MEMORANDUM

DATE:	**November 21, 1991**
TO:	**Ed Rittenhouse**
FROM:	**Marilyn St.Clair**
SUBJECT:	**Updated Salary Data**

   The following is the salary data for the Marketing, Accounting, and Sales Departments of the company.

5. Press [Return] to leave a blank line.
6. Use the **Save As** command to save the document as CHAP 11–SP.
7. Switch to the spreadsheet SP CHAP 11 from the **Window** menu.
8. Copy the block A1:F20 onto the Clipboard.
9. Switch back to the word-processing file CHAP 11–SP.
10. Choose **Paste** from the **Edit** menu.

    The spreadsheet that was on the Clipboard is pasted into the document.

11. Finish the letter.

    Would you please verify the data and inform me of any discrepancies with your records.

NOTE: You may have to change the font size of the text just entered.

12. Print the letter. It should look similar to the preview screen shown in Figure 11-2.

Figure 11-2

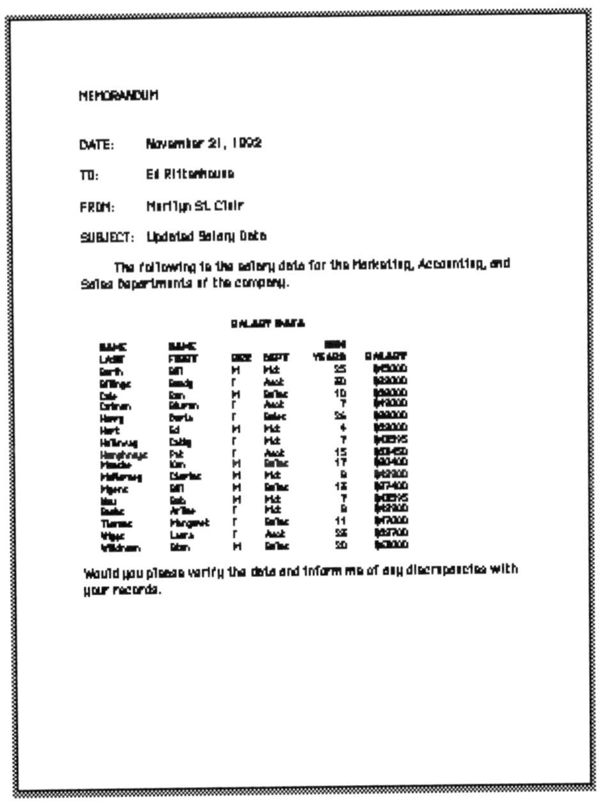

MEMORANDUM

DATE: November 21, 1992

TO: Ed Rittenhouse

FROM: Marilyn St. Clair

SUBJECT: Updated Salary Data

The following is the salary data for the Marketing, Accounting, and Sales Departments of the company.

SALARY DATA

[illegible] LAST	[illegible] FIRST	[illegible]	DEPT	YEARS	SALARY
Barth	Bill	M	Mkt	25	[illegible]
[illegible]	[illegible]	F	Acct	20	[illegible]
Cole	[illegible]	M	Sales	10	[illegible]
[illegible]	[illegible]	F	Acct	7	[illegible]
[illegible]	[illegible]	F	Sales	26	[illegible]
Hart	Ed	M	Mkt	4	[illegible]
[illegible]	[illegible]	F	Mkt	7	[illegible]
[illegible]	Pat	F	Acct	15	[illegible]
[illegible]	Kim	M	Sales	17	[illegible]
[illegible]	Charles	M	Mkt	9	[illegible]
[illegible]	Bill	M	Sales	13	[illegible]
[illegible]	Bob	M	Mkt	7	[illegible]
[illegible]	[illegible]	F	Mkt	9	[illegible]
Thomas	Margaret	F	Sales	11	[illegible]
[illegible]	Laura	F	Acct	25	[illegible]
[illegible]	[illegible]	M	Sales	20	[illegible]

Would you please verify the data and inform me of any discrepancies with your records.

MOVING INFORMATION FROM SPREADSHEET TO DATABASE

You will now transfer information in a spreadsheet file to a database file. You might recall that a spreadsheet display and a database list layout are very similar. Each row of the spreadsheet is considered to be a record of a database, and each column is a field. That is precisely how the information will be transferred. Each row will be transferred as a record in a database file, with each column being a field within the record.

First, you need to create a database whose structure corresponds to the format of the spreadsheet file. You can then transfer information. You will use the spreadsheet SP CHAP 11 created in the previous section.

1. Open a new database file.
2. Create the following fields:

FIELD	FIELD NAME
1	**LAST NAME**
2	**FIRST NAME**
3	**SEX**
4	**DEPT**
5	**YEARS**
6	**SALARY**

3. Define the last two fields as numeric, displayed in Fixed with 0 decimal places.

Now that you have a database file defined with the same structure as the spreadsheet file, you can transfer the data.

When you send information from a spreadsheet to a database, you send only the data, not the headings and other descriptive information. In the existing spreadsheet, rows 1 through 4 contain descriptive information, not the actual data. Hence you need to place information on rows 5 through 20, columns A through F, on the Clipboard.

4. Switch to the spreadsheet SP CHAP 11.
5. Copy the block A5:F20 onto the Clipboard.
6. Switch to the database file Untitled (DB).
7. Make sure that it is in the list layout.
8. Select the blank space under the field name LAST NAME.
9. Choose **Paste** from the **Edit** menu.

   The information is placed, as shown in Figure 11-3.

Figure 11-3

Untitled (DB)

LAST NAME	FIRST NAME	SEX	DEPT	YEARS	SALARY
Barth	Bill	M	Mkt	25	45000
Billings	Sandy	F	Acct	30	32000
Cole	Ron	M	Sales	10	28000
Cotman	Sharon	F	Acct	7	49000
Harry	Daria	F	Sales	26	38000
Hart	Ed	M	Mkt	4	52000
Holloway	Cathy	F	Mkt	7	43595
Humphreys	Pat	F	Acct	15	23450
Manske	Ken	M	Sales	17	30400
McNerney	Charles	M	Mkt	8	42900
Myers	Bill	M	Sales	13	37400
Nau	Bob	M	Mkt	7	43595
Sachs	Arline	F	Mkt	8	42900
Thomas	Margaret	F	Sales	11	47000
Wiggs	Laura	F	Acct	23	52700
Wilkinson	Stan	M	Sales	20	63000

10. Save the database file as DB CHAP 11.

That was easy, wasn't it?

MOVING INFORMATION FROM DATABASE TO SPREADSHEET

Moving information from database to spreadsheet is just as simple. Information in a database record is transferred to a row in the spreadsheet, with the content of each field transferred to a column of the spreadsheet. Even the row headings are created from the field names.

1. Make sure that you are in the database file DB CHAP 11.
2. Select the entire file by choosing **Select All** from the **Edit** menu.
3. Copy onto the Clipboard.
4. Open a new spreadsheet file.
5. Select cell A1.
6. Choose **Paste** from the **Edit** menu.

   The information from the database file appears on the screen.

MOVING INFORMATION FROM DATABASE TO WORD PROCESSOR

This is similar to including spreadsheet information in a word-processing document. Again, place the database information on the Clipboard. Then, as you type the document, paste the information from the Clipboard at the appropriate place.

1. Switch to the database file DB CHAP 11.
2. Install the Record Selection Rule DEPT = Sales and select.

   Six records are displayed on the list layout.
3. Select all, then copy onto the Clipboard.
4. Open a new word-processing file.
5. Type the following document. The document is incomplete.

June 25, 1992

Carol Noonkester
Equal Employment Opportunities Board
P.O. Box 10110
San Francisco, CA 95926

Dear Ms. Noonkester:

The report on company salaries for the Sales Department is as follows:

6. Insert a blank line.
7. Choose **Paste** from the **Edit** menu.

   The document looks similar to the one shown in Figure 11-4.

Figure 11-4

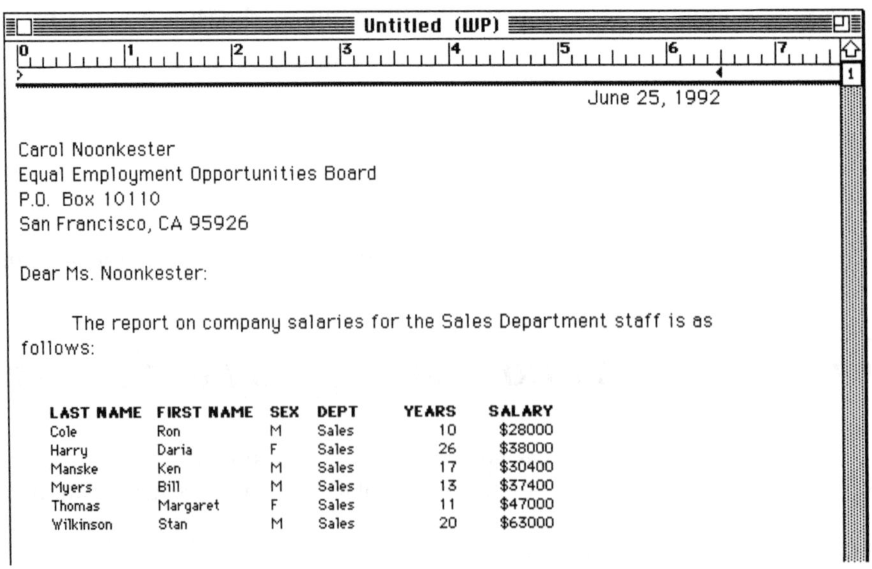

Untitled (WP)

June 25, 1992

Carol Noonkester
Equal Employment Opportunities Board
P.O. Box 10110
San Francisco, CA 95926

Dear Ms. Noonkester:

The report on company salaries for the Sales Department staff is as follows:

LAST NAME	FIRST NAME	SEX	DEPT	YEARS	SALARY
Cole	Ron	M	Sales	10	$28000
Harry	Daria	F	Sales	26	$38000
Manske	Ken	M	Sales	17	$30400
Myers	Bill	M	Sales	13	$37400
Thomas	Margaret	F	Sales	11	$47000
Wilkinson	Stan	M	Sales	20	$63000

8. Insert two blank lines below the database information.
9. Continue the document with the following text:

If you have any questions, please contact me.

Sincerely,

Marilyn St.Clair

10. Save the document on the data disk as file CHAP 11–DB.

MERGING INFORMATION IN THE DATABASE INTO A WORD-PROCESSING DOCUMENT

There are times when you need to send the same memo to different people, all of whom are in a database file. The merge feature becomes very useful—merging information in a database with a document in a word-processing file.

You will use the database file DB CHAP 11 and insert name, number of years, and salary into a word-processing document. To indicate where information from a database is to be inserted into a word-processing document, **placeholders** are used. These contain the name of the database and the field containing the data to be printed in that position. The Prepare to Merge command is used to insert the placeholder.

1. Open a new word-processing file.
2. Type the following:

MEMORANDUM

DATE: **December 14, 1992**

TO:

NOTE: Make sure that you've pressed Tab *after typing TO: so that the cursor is placed where you want the name to appear.*

You are now ready to enter a name from the database file.

3. Choose the **Prepare to Merge** command from the **Edit** menu.

   The Prepare to Merge dialog box is displayed, as shown in Figure 11-5.

Since the DB CHAP 11 database file is the only one open on the desktop, it is the selected database file. In the right box, the fields in the DB CHAP 11 database appear. You want to include the person's first name and last name.

Figure 11-5

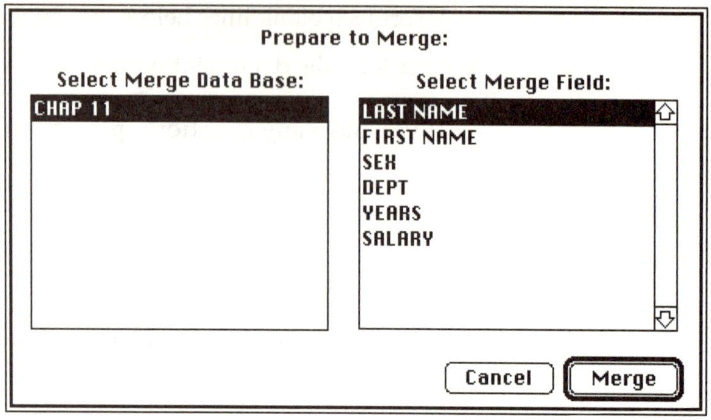

4. Click on the field **FIRST NAME**.
5. Click on the **Merge** button.

   Works displays information from the first record (Ron). However, a placeholder for the FIRST NAME field of the database file DB CHAP 11 was inserted.

6. Press Spacebar once to insert a blank space.
7. Choose **Prepare to Merge** from the **Edit** menu.
8. Click on the **LAST NAME** field.
9. Click on the **Merge** button.

   Although the last name Cole appears in the document, a placeholder for the last name was inserted.

10. Continue with the memo, inserting the appropriate placeholders where indicated.

    FROM: **Marilyn St.Clair**

    SUBJECT: **Report to Equal Employment Opportunities Board**

    We were recently asked to report your current salary and the number of years you've worked for the company to the Equal Employment Opportunities Board. The following information was supplied.

    Salary: **<PLACEHOLDER FOR SALARY>**

    Number of years: **<PLACEHOLDER FOR NUMBER OF YEARS>**

    If you have any questions, please contact me.

    The screen should look similar to Figure 11-6.

Figure 11-6

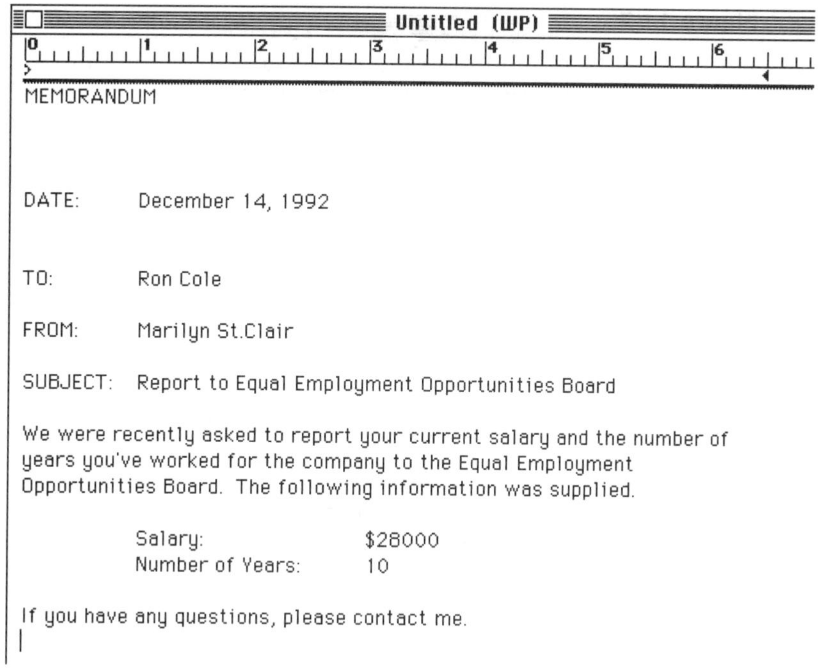

Untitled (WP)

MEMORANDUM

DATE: December 14, 1992

TO: Ron Cole

FROM: Marilyn St.Clair

SUBJECT: Report to Equal Employment Opportunities Board

We were recently asked to report your current salary and the number of years you've worked for the company to the Equal Employment Opportunities Board. The following information was supplied.

Salary: $28000
Number of Years: 10

If you have any questions, please contact me.

You can look at the placeholders that were actually inserted.

1. Choose **Show Field Names** from the **Edit** menu.

   The screen should look similar to Figure 11-7 on the following page.

To display the data from the first record,

2. Choose **Show Field Data** from the **Edit** menu.

   The screen returns to displaying the contents of the first record.

3. Save the document as CHAP 11–MERGE on the data disk.

Since you only reported salaries for people in the Sales Department, you must select only those records from the database file.

1. Switch to the database file DB CHAP 11.

   The Record Selection Rule for DEPT = Sales installed earlier is still in effect.

2. Switch back to the file CHAP 11–MERGE.

3. Print the document by choosing the **Print Merge** command from the **File** menu. Make sure that the **Preview** option is selected.

   The first document is displayed.

Figure 11-7

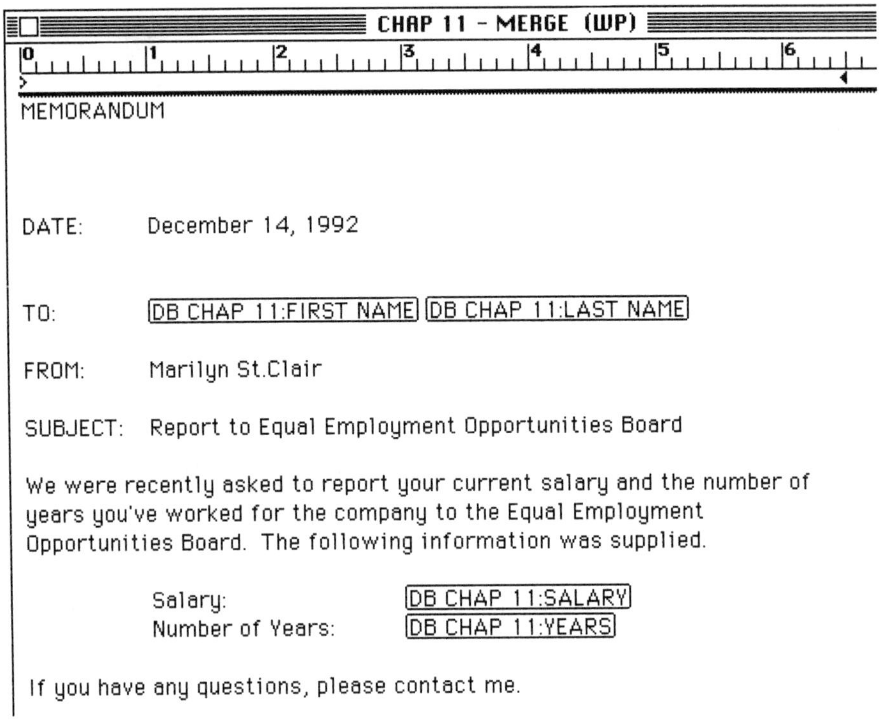
CHAP 11 - MERGE (WP)

MEMORANDUM

DATE: December 14, 1992

TO: DB CHAP 11:FIRST NAME DB CHAP 11:LAST NAME

FROM: Marilyn St.Clair

SUBJECT: Report to Equal Employment Opportunities Board

We were recently asked to report your current salary and the number of years you've worked for the company to the Equal Employment Opportunities Board. The following information was supplied.

Salary: DB CHAP 11:SALARY
Number of Years: DB CHAP 11:YEARS

If you have any questions, please contact me.

4. Click on the **Next** button.

   The second document is displayed.

As you click on the Next button, you will note that six personalized memos were created.

5. Click on the **Cancel** button.

This is the end of this lesson. Quit Works as described in Lesson One. Saving the changes is optional.

■ SUMMARY

Topic or Feature	*Command or Reference*	*Menu*	*Page*
Select the Entire File	Select All	Edit	125
Position Placeholder for Merge Field	Prepare to Merge	Edit	127
Show Placeholders in a Merge Document	Show Field Names	Edit	129

Topic or Feature	*Command or Reference*	*Menu*	*Page*
Show Values from the First Record in a Merge Document	Show Field Data	Edit	129
Print Merged Document	Print Merge	File	129

■ SELF-TEST

1. To include information from a spreadsheet or database in a word-processing document, that information is first placed on the ______________.
2. When you select spreadsheet rows to transfer information into a database file, you do not want to include ______________.
3. A database file that is to receive information from a spreadsheet must be defined with ______________ (fields/records) that correspond to the columns in the spreadsheet.
4. When you copy and paste information from the database into a spreadsheet, the column headings are ______________ automatically.
5. In a merge operation, the placeholder for a merge field is inserted through the ______________ command from the ______________ menu.
6. When you first put a placeholder for a merge field in a document, ______________ is displayed on the document.
7. Placeholders can be displayed in a merge document by choosing the ______________ command from the ______________ menu.
8. A merged document is printed using the ______________ command from the ______________ menu.

Self-Test Answers

LESSON 1

1. 14
2. click
3. point, hold down the mouse, drag, and release
4. double-click
5. default
6. Drive
7. Untitled
8. Save As
9. upper-left
10. disk

LESSON 2

1. I-beam
2. paragraph, blank line
3. insertion bar
4. positioning the pointer at the beginning of the text, and dragging the mouse
5. Clipboard
6. cut, copy
7. Paste
8. replaces
9. File
10. cannot

LESSON 3

1. Page Setup
2. left indent
3. Ruler Line
4. first line
5. clicking the mouse on the Ruler Line
6. dragging the tab marker off the Ruler Line
7. both
8. Window
9. Style, Format
10. anywhere in, Copy Format

LESSON 4

1. Clipboard
2. is not
3. right
4. right
5. the decimal point
6. Match Whole Words Only
7. Replace All
8. soft page breaks
9. Insert Page Break, Format
10. footer

LESSON 5

1. active
2. Find Cell, Select
3. clicking on the enter box, pressing Return, Tab, Shift-Tab, or Shift-Return.
4. a letter (A to Z)
5. equals sign (=)
6. *
7. 4
8. pointing
9. Clear, Edit
10. Print, File

LESSON 6

1. =B1 + B2
2. number signs (#)
3. the right edge of the column heading
4. Column Width, Format
5. Full Right, Edit
6. =SUM(B1,C1:C3)
7. Paste Function
8. A1:A4
9. written over
10. 11

LESSON 7

1. Select All, Edit
2. Set Cell Attributes
3. toggle
4. the results of formulas
5. Clipboard
6. remains intact
7. cut, copy, paste
8. cutting
9. Sort, Edit
10. ascending

LESSON 8

1. fields
2. Set Field Attributes, Format
3. cancel the entry (abort)
4. Return
5. pointing to the right edge of the entry box and dragging to the right
6. list
7. cross
8. type the entry
9. Print Window, File
10. Find Field, Organize

LESSON 9

1. click on that field
2. do not
3. Record Selection, Organize
4. AND
5. balance is greater than or equal to 100 AND is less than or equal to 200
6. field name
7. hand
8. before
9. Clipboard
10. Cut, Edit

LESSON 10

1. Change Report Title, Edit
2. database
3. margins
4. a header
5. &c&b
6. Selection, Record Selection, Organize
7. smaller
8. 2.5
9. Sum This Field, TotalPage
10. remain intact

LESSON 11

1. Clipboard
2. descriptive information
3. fields
4. inserted
5. Prepare to Merge, Edit
6. field content from the first record
7. Show Field Names, Edit
8. Print Merge, File

Works 2.0 for the Mac Command Summary

COMMON TASKS

Launch Microsoft Works
Double-click on MS Works icon.

Create a New File
From the Open dialog box,
1. Click on the icon for an application tool.
2. Click on **New**.

or

From the **File** menu,
1. Choose **New**.
2. Click on the icon for an application tool.
3. Click **OK**.

Open a File
From the Open dialog box,
1. Select a filename.
2. Click **Open**.

or

From the **File** menu,
1. Choose **Open**.
2. Select a filename.
3. Click **Open**.

Close a File
Choose **Close** from the **File** menu.

or

Click on the close box.

Delete a file
1. Choose **Delete** from the **File** menu.
2. Select a file from the list box.
3. Click **Delete**.
4. Click **OK**.

Save a File with a New Name
1. From the **File** menu, choose **Save As**.
2. Type a filename.
3. Click **Save**.

Save a File with the Same Name
From the **File** menu, choose **Save**.

Switch Between Files
From the **Window** menu, choose the filename.

Help
1. From the **Window** menu, choose **Help**.
   The pointer changes to a question mark when outside the Help window.
2. Choose the command you want help with.
3. When finished, click the close box in the **Help** window.

Quit Microsoft Works
From the **File** menu, choose **Quit**.

PRINTING A FILE

Print a File
1. From the **File** menu, choose **Print**.
2. Choose the options you want.
3. Click **OK** or **Print**.

Print a File Horizontally
1. From the **File** menu, choose **Page Setup**.
2. Under Orientation, click the icon for horizontal printing.
3. Click **OK**.
4. Follow the steps to print a file.

Print a Window
From the **File** menu, choose **Print Window**.

Preview Before Printing
1. From the **File** menu, choose **Print**.
2. Click **Print Preview**.
3. Click **OK** or **Print**.
4. Preview the document.
   To enlarge the page, move the pointer over the page. Click when the pointer becomes a magnifying glass. When you click, the pointer becomes a hand. To move the page, drag with the hand.

To reduce the page to its original size, double-click.
To view other pages, click **Previous** and **Next**.
5. To print the document, click **Print**.

WORD PROCESSOR COMMANDS

Select Text

- **a character**, drag across it.
- **a word**, double-click it.
- **a line**, click in the blank area to the left of the line when the pointer changes to an arrow.
- **a paragraph**, double-click in the blank area to the left of the paragraph when the pointer changes to an arrow.
- **a section of text**, drag across it.

Copy Text

1. Select text.
2. From the **Edit** menu, choose **Copy**.
3. Position the insertion bar where you want text moved.
4. From the **Edit** menu, choose **Paste**.

Delete Text

1. Place insertion bar to the right of error.
2. Press Delete.

or

1. Select text.
2. Press Delete.

Find Text

1. From the **Search** menu, choose **Find**.
2. In the **Find What** box, type the text you want to find.
3. Click the appropriate options.
4. Click **Find Next**.

Find and Replace Text

1. From the **Search** menu, choose **Replace**.
2. In the **Find What** box, type the text you want to replace.
3. In the **Replace With** box, type the text you want to replace it with.
4. Click the appropriate options.
5. Click a button.
   - Click **Find Next** to find the first occurrence, but not replace it.
   - Click **Replace**, then **Find**, to change the currently selected occurrence and find the next one.
   - Click **Replace All** to change every occurrence.

Insert Text

1. Place the insertion bar where you want text inserted.
2. Type text.

Move Text

1. Select text.
2. From the **Edit** menu, choose **Cut**.
3. Position the insertion bar where you want text moved.
4. From the **Edit** menu, choose **Paste**.

Move or Copy Text to Another Document

1. Select text.
2. From the **Edit** menu, choose **Cut** or **Copy**.
3. From the **Window** menu, choose another file.
4. Position insertion bar where you want the text moved or copied.
5. From the **Edit** menu, choose **Paste**.

Replace Text

1. Select text to be replaced.
2. Type the new text.

Check Your Spelling

From the **Spell** menu, choose **Correct Spelling**.

Insert a Hard Page Break

1. Position the insertion bar where you want to begin a new page.
2. From the **Format** menu, choose **Insert Page Break**.

Copy Format

1. Position the insertion bar in the paragraph whose format you want to copy.
2. From the **Format** menu, choose **Copy Format**.
3. Move the insertion bar to the paragraph you want to format.
4. From the **Format** menu, choose **Paste Format**.

For the following format specifications, you can select a block of text and give the command, or enter the command, then type the text.

Bold or Underline

1. From the **Format** menu, choose **Style**.
2. Drag to choose **Bold** or **Underline**.

Font

1. From the **Format** menu, choose **Font**.
2. Drag to choose the desired font.

Justification
1. From the **Format** menu, choose **Justification.**
2. Drag to choose the desired justification.

Size
1. From the **Format** menu, choose **Size**.
2. Drag to choose the desired size.

Spacing
1. From the **Format** menu, choose **Spacing**.
2. Drag to choose the desired spacing.

Tabs
1. Place the pointer on the Ruler Line where tab is to be set.
2. For a right tab, click twice; for a left tab, click once; and for a decimal tab, click three times.

Text Width/Indentation of Text Relative to Left Margin
1. Make sure that the Ruler Line is displayed. If not, choose **Show Ruler** from the **Format** menu.
2. Drag the appropriate indent marker on the Ruler Line.

SPREADSHEET COMMANDS

Select
- **a cell**, click it.
- **the last cell**, choose **Last Cell** from the **Select** menu.
- **a column**, click the column heading.
- **a row**, click the row heading.
- **a range of cells**, drag across it.
- **several columns**, drag across the column headings.
- **several rows**, drag across the row headings.
- **all cells** in the spreadsheet, choose **Select All** from the **Edit** menu.
- **all cells from A1 to the last cell**, choose **All Cells** from the **Select** menu.

Find a Cell
1. From the **Select** menu, choose **Find Cell.**
2. Type cell address.
3. Click **OK**.

Enter Text
1. Select a cell.
2. Start the entry with a letter (A-Z) or a quotation mark (").

Enter Numbers
1. Select a cell.
2. Start the entry with a number, a decimal point, a plus sign (+), or a minus sign (–).

Enter Formulas
1. Select a cell.
2. Start the entry with an equals sign (=).

NOTE: Enter cell references by typing or by clicking the cell or range of cells.
Functions can be typed or pasted from the Paste Function command in the Edit menu.

Complete an Entry
- Click the enter box to leave the cell selection where it is.
- Press [Tab] to select the cell on the right.
- Press [Shift]-[Tab] to select the cell on the left.
- Press [Return] to select the cell below.
- Press [Shift]-[Return] to select the cell above.

Erase Entries in a Range of Cells
1. Select a range whose content you want to erase.
2. From the **Edit** menu, choose **Clear**.

Insert a Row or a Column
1. Select row or column where you want the new row or column.
2. From the **Edit** menu, choose **Insert**.

Copy Cell Content
1. Select across row or column you want to copy from and the area you want to copy contents to.
2. From the **Edit** menu, choose **Fill Right** to copy across a row *or* choose **Fill Down** to copy down a column.

Change Column Width
1. Select column(s).
2. From the **Format** menu, choose **Column Width.**
3. Specify the desired column width.

or

1. Point to the right edge of the column heading. Pointer changes to a cross.
2. Drag the mouse.

Move Range to Another Location
1. Select range to be moved.
2. From the **Edit** menu, choose **Cut**.
3. If the destination is another spreadsheet, choose the filename from the **Window** menu.
4. Select the cell which is the top right corner of the destination range.
5. From the **Edit** menu, choose **Paste**.

Remove Row(s) or Column(s)
1. Select row(s) or column(s) to be deleted.

2. From the **Edit** menu, choose **Cut**.

Display Formulas

From the **Options** menu, choose **Show Formulas**.

Arrange Rows

1. Select the cells you want to sort.
2. From the **Edit** menu, choose **Sort**.
3. Type the column heading of the first key column to sort on.
4. Click a sorting order.
5. If you have a second or third key column, move the insertion point into the appropriate box and type the column heading.
6. Click **OK**.

Cell Attributes

1. Select a cell.
2. From the **Format** menu, choose **Set Cell Attributes**.
   Specify the following field attributes:
   Type — Text, Numeric, Date, Time
   Display — General, Fixed, Dollar, Percent, Scientific
   Alignment — left, center, or right justification
   Style — bold, underline, commas
   Number of decimal places
3. Click the appropriate options.
4. Click **OK**.

Print Selected Cells

1. Select the cells you want to print.
2. From the **File** menu, choose **Print**.
3. Fill out the dialog box and click **OK** or **Print**.

DATABASE COMMANDS

Select

- **an entry** in a list window, click the entry.
- **a field** in a list or form window, click the field name.
- **an entire record** in a list window, click the record selector box.
- **a block of entries** in a list window, drag across the entries or record selector boxes.

NOTE: The record selector box is the empty box to the left of the record in the list window.

Cancel a Selection

Click the deselect box (in the upper-left corner of the list window).

Set Up a New Database and Name Fields

1. Create a database document.
2. Type the name of the first field.
3. Click on **Add Field**.
4. Add more fields as needed.
5. Click **Done** when you are finished adding fields.

Specify a Field as Numeric

1. Select the field.
2. From the **Format** menu, choose **Set Field Attributes**.
3. Click on **Numeric**.
4. Click **OK**.

Make an Entry

1. Select a field.
2. Type the information.
3. Click on the enter box to leave the selection in the same box. When making an entry from the list layout, press [Tab] to move the selection to the next field in the same record or [Return] to move the selection to the same field in the next record. When making an entry in the form layout, press [Tab] to move the selection horizontally to the next field, or [Return] to move the selection vertically to the next field in the same record.

Cancel an Entry

Click the cancel box.

Display in Form Layout

From the **Format** menu, choose **Show Form**.

Display in List Layout

From the **Format** menu, choose **Show List**.

Adjust Field Width in the Form Layout

1. Position pointer on the right edge of the box.
2. Drag.

Change Field Width in the List Layout

1. Position pointer on the line between columns in the list layout.
   The pointer turns into a cross.
2. Drag.

Move a Field in the Form Layout

1. Position the pointer on the field name.
   The pointer turns into a hand.
2. Drag the field to its new position.

Change Field Display Order in the List Layout

1. Place pointer on the field name to move.
   The pointer turns into a hand.
2. Drag.

Add a Field

From the **Edit** menu, choose **Add New Field**.

Delete a Field

1. Select the field to be deleted.

2. From the **Edit** menu, choose **Delete Field.**

Insert a Record

1. Select a record to follow the new record.
2. From the **Edit** menu, choose **Insert Record.**

Copy a Record

1. Select fields to copy.
2. From the **Edit** menu, choose **Copy.**
3. Select position to copy to.
4. From the **Edit** menu, choose **Paste.**

Delete a Record

1. Select the record.
2. From the **Edit** menu, choose **Cut.**

Set Field Attributes

1. Select a field.
2. From the **Format** menu, choose **Set Field Attributes.**
   Specify the following field attributes:
   Type — Text, Numeric, Date, Time
   Display — General, Fixed, Dollar, Percent, Scientific
   Alignment — left, center, or right justification
   Style — bold, underline, commas
   Number of decimal places
3. Click the appropriate options.
4. Click **OK.**

Print a Form

1. Display the record in the form layout.
2. From the **File** menu, choose **Print Window.**

Find a Record

1. From the **Organize** menu, choose **Find Field.**
2. Type the information you want Works to look for.
3. Click **Find Next.**

Arrange Records

1. Click a field name or select any entries in a field to specify the field to sort on.
2. From the **Organize** menu, choose **Sort.**
3. Click the order you want.
4. Click **OK.**

Record Selection

1. From the **Organize** menu, choose **Record Selection.**
2. Select a field name.
3. Select a comparison phrase.
4. Type the record comparison information in the text box.
5. Click the **Install Rule** button.
6. Click **Select.**

Multiple Selection Rule

1. From the **Organize** menu, choose **Record Selection.**
2. Select a field name.
3. Select a comparison phrase.
4. Type the record comparison information in the text box.
5. Click the **Install Rule** button.
6. Choose a connector.
7. Repeat steps 2 through 6 as necessary.
8. Click **Select.**

Define a New Report

1. From the **Report** menu, choose **New Report.**
2. Print the report or close the report window to store the report definition with the database file.

Define Which Records to Include in the Report

In the Report window, choose **Record Selection** from the **Organize** menu.

Define What Fields to Include in the Report

1. In the Report window, arrange the fields in the order you want them printed.
2. Move or size fields, then drag the right margin marker so that only those fields you want are contained within the report margins.

Display Total

1. In the Report window, select a numeric field.
2. From the **TotalPage** menu, choose **Sum This Field.**

Change Report Title

From the **Edit** menu, choose **Change Report Title.**

Copy a Report Definition

1. From the **Report** menu, choose **Duplicate Report.**
2. Click the name of the report definition you want.
3. Click **OK.**

MERGE COMMANDS

Position Placeholder for Merge Field

1. Position the insertion bar where you want to insert a placeholder.
2. From the **Edit** menu, choose **Prepare to Merge.**
3. Select the database file you want to use.
4. Select a field to merge.
5. Click **Merge.**

Show Placeholders in a Merge Document

From the **Edit** menu, choose **Show Field Names.**

Show Values from the First Record in a Merge Document
From the **Edit** menu, choose **Show Field Data**.

Print Merged Document
From the **File** menu, choose **Print Merge**.

Works 2.0 for the Mac Keyboard Commands

Many commands can be invoked by holding down ⌘ and pressing the letter corresponding to the particular command. The following table lists the keyboard commands for word processing, spreadsheet, and database.

Key	*Word Processing*	*Spreadsheet*	*Database*
A		Absolute Cell Reference/Relative Cell Reference	Sort
B	Bold	Bold	
C	Copy	Copy	Copy
D		Fill Down	Enter Date
F	Find	Find Cell	Find Field
G	Go to Page Number	Go to Cell	
I	Italic	Insert	Insert Record
J	Draw On/Off	Draw On/Off	
K	Copy Format		
L			Show List/Form
M	Prepare to Merge		Match Records
N	Normal Text	Normal Text	
O	Open	Open	Open
P	Print	Print	Print
Q	Quit	Quit	Quit
R	Replace	Fill Right	
S	Save	Save	Save
T			Enter Time
U	Underline	Underline	
V	Paste	Paste	Paste
W	Close	Close	Close
X	Cut	Cut	Cut
Y	Paste Format		
Z	Undo	Undo	Undo
=		Calculate Now	
?	Help	Help	Help

Index

A

Absolute reference, 63
Active cell, 51–52, 55
Add Field button, 84–85, 95, 118
Add New Field, 118–120
Align characters
  left margin, 47
  right margin, 47
Alphabetic order, 79–80, 98
And, selection rule, 102
Application icons, 4, 10, 50
Arithmetic operators, 56
Arrange records, 98–99, 107
Arrange rows, 78–81
Ascending order, 80
Attributes
  cell, 72–75, 80–81
  field, 84–86, 95

B

&b command, 47, 112
Backspace key, 85. *See also* Delete, key
Bar
  Menu, 2–3
  Scroll, 2
  Title, 2
Begins with, 100
Blank entry form, 88
Blank line, creating, 18
Bold characters, 35–36, 72–73, 80
Box width, 87
Buttons, active, 5

C

&c command, 47, 112
Cancel button, 54, 86, 113–114, 130
Cancel printing, 9, 59
Caps Lock key, 18, 53
Cell
  attributes, 73
  defined, 50
  indicator, 51
  reference, 67
  select, 59
Center
  characters, 47
  tab alignment, 33
  text, 34–35
Change
  disk, 5
  display format, 72–75
  field, 107
  folder, 5
  Report Title, 110, 119
  spreadsheet display format, 72–75
Change Report Title command, 110, 119
Clear command, 55, 57, 59
Click, 3, 14
Clipboard, 20–21, 39–40, 75–76, 78, 105–106, 123–126
Close
  Box, 2
  command, 10, 14
  file, 10
Columns, 50, 76
Column width, 52, 63–67, 70
Command-B keystroke, 36
Command key, 13
Command-U keystroke, 36
Commands, summary of, 14, 24–25, 37–38, 48, 59–60, 70–71, 80–81, 107–108, 119–120, 130–131
Condition scroll box, 102
Connector, 102
Constant values, 53
Coordinates, active cell, 51
Copy
  cell contents, 70

Copy *(continued)*
  command, 21
  Format command, 37
  record, 105–107
  text, 21, 24
Correct errors, 18, 55, 59
Correct Spelling command, 22–23
Create file, 5–6
Current disk, 5
Cut command, 20, 24, 48, 75–76

D

&d command, 47, 112
Database (DB)
  arrange records, 98–99
  change box width, 87
  connector, 102
  copy records, 105–106
  correct errors, 88
  create file, 83–90
  delete record, 106–107
  field display order, 103–104
  field display width, 92
  field names, 84–85
  find information, 93–94
  form layout, 91–92
  insert record, 104–105
  list layout, 91–92, 95, 104
  merge data in word processor, 126–130
  move data to spreadsheet, 125
  move data to word processor, 125–126
  multiple selection rule, 101–102, 107
  numeric field, 85–86
  numeric range selection, 102–103
  print record, 92–93, 95
  quick save, 107
  records, 84, 86–90, 92–93, 95
  save file, 90–91
  select record, 92–93, 99–101, 107
  text field, 84–85
  Title Bar, 6, 83
  update, 94
Data disk, 6
Date, print, 47
DB. *See* Database
Decimal places, 74–75
Decimal tab alignment, 33, 42–43
Default settings
  defined, 5
  margins, 28
  printer, 9
  spreadsheet, 70
Delete
  block of text, 20
  character, 19, 24
  columns, 76
  command, 14
  Field command, 119–120
  file, 11–12
  key, 18, 86, 88
  record, 106–107
  Rule button, 100–101
  text, 18–20
Descending order, 80
Desktop, 1–2
Dialog box
  Change Report Title, 110, 119
  delete, 11–12
  Field Name, 84
  Find Field, 93
  open, 4–5, 121
  Page Setup, 27–29, 111, 117
  Paste Function, 67–68
  Prepare to Merge, 127–128
  Print, 113
  Record Selection, 115
  Report Title, 110
  Save As, 90–91
  Set Cell Attributes, 73
  Set Field Attributes, 85–86
  Sort, 79–80
Dictionary, 22
Dimmed buttons, 5
Disk drives
  change, 5
  current, 5
  eject disk from, 5
  start from, 4
Display format, change, 72–75
Display order of records, 107
Display total, 117–118, 120
Document. *See* Word processing
Dollar sign, 63
Double-click, 3, 14
Drag, 3
Duplicate Report command, 114–115, 119

E

Editing documents. *See also* Word processing
Change Report Title, 110
copy format, 43–44
cut and paste, 39–40
page breaks, 46–47
page numbering, 47
replace words, 44–46
right justified text, 40–42
tab alignment, 42–43
Editing spreadsheets
change display format, 72–75
cut and paste, 75–76
delete columns, 76
formula display, 77
move data between spreadsheets, 78
sort rows, 78–80
Edit menu
Add New Field, 118–119
Change Report Title, 119
Clear, 55, 57, 60
Copy, 21, 24, 40, 48, 78, 105–106
Cut, 20, 24, 48, 75–76, 78, 81, 106
Delete Field command, 119–120
Fill Down, 68
Fill Right, 62–63, 70
Insert, 62, 70
Insert Record, 104–105, 107
Paste, 21, 24, 40, 48, 105–106, 123–125
Paste function, 67, 70, 76, 78, 81
Prepare to Merge, 127, 130
Select All, 74, 80, 125, 130
Show Field Data, 131
Show Field Names, 129–130
Sort, 79–81
Eject button, 5, 7
Enter box, 54, 86
Enter key, 55
Entry bar, 51, 54, 85
Equals condition, 100, 102
Equals sign, 56, 68
Escape key, 88

F

Features, Works 2.0
close file, 10
create new file, 5–6
database, 83–120
delete file, 11–12
desktop, 1–2
Help screen, 12–13
keyboard commands, 13
Menu Bar, 2–3, 83
Mouse commands, 2–3
open file from disk, 10–11
print file, 8–9
quit, 13
save file, 6–8
spreadsheet, 50–82
start up, 3–5
switch between desktop files, 9–10
word processing, 16–49
Field
attributes, 84–86, 95
change, 107
delete, 119
display order, 107
display width, 92
Field Data, 129–130
Find, 93, 95, 99
insert, 118–119
Name dialog box, 84
names, 84–85
report with selected, 115–117
scroll box, 102
Show Field Names, 129
Sum This, 117
File
close, 2, 10
create new, 5–6, 16
defined, 2
delete, 11–12
open, 2
open from disk, 10–11
print, 8–9
retrieve, 10–11
save, 6–8
switch, 9–10
File menu
Close, 10
Delete, 11
New, 5–6, 78
Open, 10–11
Page Setup, 27–29, 37, 47–48, 69–71, 111
Preview option, 129
Print, 8–9, 58, 60, 77, 113
Print Merge, 129, 131

File menu *(continued)*
  Print Window, 93
  Quit, 13–14
  Save, 8, 58, 60, 90–91
  Save As, 7, 19, 58, 60, 69, 90–91
Filename, 6
Fill Down command, 68
Fill Right command, 62–63, 70
Find
  Cell command, 52–53, 59
  command, 43–44, 48
  Field command, 93–95, 99
  Field dialog box, 93
  Next button, 44, 46, 53, 93–94
First line indent marker, 29–32
Fixed format, 74–75
Folder, 5
Font, 36
Footers, 37
Format menu
  Column Width, 63–67, 70
  Copy Format, 37
  Font, 36–37
  Insert Page Break, 46–48
  Justification, 34–35, 37, 48
  overview of options, 27
  Set Cell Attributes, 72–75, 80–81
  Set Field Attributes, 85–86, 95
  Show Form, 92–95, 104–105
  Show List, 91, 93–95
  Show Ruler, 29, 37
  Size, 36–37, 116, 120
  Spacing, 36–37
  Style, 35–37
Formatting a document. *See also* Word processing
  bold characters, 35–36
  copy format, 37
  font, 36
  justification, 34–35
  line indentation, 30–31
  line spacing, 36–37
  page setup, 27–29
  paragraphs, 31–32
  Ruler Line, 29
  size of characters, 36
  tab alignment, 32–33
  underline text, 35–36
Form layout, 91–92, 99
Formulas, 56–59, 62–63, 77
Function, 67, 71

H

Hanging paragraph, 31–32
Hard disk drive, starting from, 3
Hard page breaks, 46–48
Header box, 112
Headers, 37, 47
Help command, 12–14
Hide Clipboard command, 40
Highlight text, 20, 24
Horizontal orientation icon, 111
Horizontal scroll bar, 91

I

I-beam, 2, 17, 20
Icon
  application, 4
  defined, 2
  Microsoft Works, 3
  word processor, 16
ImageWriter printer, 9, 23, 28–29, 59, 112–113
Indent markers, 17, 29–32
Insert
  command, 61–62, 70
  field, 118–119
  record, 104–105, 107
  row, 61–62, 70
  text, 21–22, 24
Insertion bar, 17, 19–21, 27
Install Rule button, 102–103

J

Justification, 34–35, 40–42, 48
Justifying text entry, 73–74

K

Keyboard commands, 13

L

&l command, 47, 112
Label, 2, 53
LaserWriter printer, 9, 24, 28, 59, 112–113
Left-edge marker, 110
Left indent marker, 29–32

Left tab alignment, 33, 42
Line indentation, 30–31
Line spacing, 36–37
List box, 5
List layout, 91–92, 95, 104

M

Margin settings, 28–29, 37
Markers, indent, 29–32
Mathematical operations, 56
Menu Bar
- database, 83–86
- defined, 2
- spreadsheet, 50–51
- word processor, 16–17

Merge button, 128
Merge data, 126–130
Microsoft Works icon, 3
Mouse
- click, 3, 14
- double-click, 3, 14
- drag, 3
- pointer, 2
- select, 3

Move
- data between spreadsheets, 78, 81
- data from database to spreadsheet, 125
- data from database to word processor, 125–126
- data from spreadsheet to database, 123–125
- data from spreadsheet to word processor, 121–123
- fields, 119
- text, 20–21, 24

MsWorksDict file, 22
Multiple selection rule, 101–102, 107

N

New button
- spreadsheet, 50
- word processor, 16

New command, 5–6, 78
New Report command, 119
Numbers, spreadsheet, 55–56, 59, 74–75
Number sign (#), 65
Numeric field, 85
Numeric range selection, 102–103

O

Open
- command, 14
- dialog box, 4–5, 121
- file, 10–11, 26

Operators, 56
Options menu
- Show Formulas, 77, 81
- Show Values, 77

Or, selection rule, 102
Order of operations, arithmetic, 56
Organize menu
- Find Field, 93–95, 99
- Record Selection, 100–103, 115, 119
- Show All Records, 100
- Sort, 98–99, 107, 117

Orientation, printing, 70
Outdenting, 31–32

P

&p command, 47, 112
Page
- breaks, 46–48
- numbering, 47
- orientation, 70
- Setup command, 27–29, 37, 47, 69–71, 111
- Setup dialog box, 27, 69–70, 111, 117

Paging, 46–47
Paper size, 27–29, 37
Paragraph indentation, 16–17, 31–32
Paste
- command, 21, 40, 123–125
- function, 67, 70
- function dialog box, 67–68

Point, 3
Pointer, mouse, 3, 12
Prepare to Merge command, 127–128
Print
- bold characters, 47
- button, 113
- command, 14, 58, 60, 77, 113
- database form, 93, 95
- date, 47
- dialog box, 8–9, 23–24, 58, 113
- file, 8–9, 23–25, 37
- horizontal orientation, 69–70
- Merge command, 129

Print *(continued)*
- page number, 47
- Preview option, 113, 129
- size, 120
- spreadsheet, 58–59, 69–70, 77

Print Window, 93, 95
Pull-down menu, 2

Q

Question mark pointer, 12
Quit command, 13–14
Quotation mark, in spreadsheet, 53

R

&r command, 47, 112
RAM. *See* Random Access Memory
Random Access Memory (RAM), 2, 6
Range, reference, 67
Record. *See also* Database
- alphabetical order, 98–99
- arrange, 98–99, 107
- copy, 105–107
- defined, 84
- delete, 106–107
- display order, 107
- enter, 86–90
- field display width, 92
- field names, 84–85
- Find Field command, 93–95
- form layout, 91, 95
- insert, 104–105, 107
- list layout, 91–92, 95, 104
- multiple selection rule, 101–102, 107
- numerical order, 98–99
- print, 92–93, 95
- select, 92–93, 99–103
- Selection command, 99–102, 107, 115, 119
- sort, 98–99, 107
- update, 94

Relative reference, 63
Removing file, 11–12
Replace
- All button, 46
- command, 22, 45–46, 48
- text, 21–22, 24
- words, 44–46

Report. *See also* Database
- Add New Field, 118–119
- change database structure, 118–119
- change title, 110
- defined, 109–114
- define new, 119
- display total, 117–118
- Duplicate, 114–115
- edge markers, 110
- formatting, 109–114
- New, 119
- Ruler Line, 110
- Save, 114
- Select, 114, 117
- selected fields, 115–117
- selected records, 114–115
- Set Field Attributes command, 85–86, 95
- Sum This Field, 117
- Title dialog box, 110
- totals, 117

Report menu
- Duplicate, 114–115
- New Report, 110, 119
- Select Report, 114

Report Title dialog box, 110
Retrieving file, 10–11, 26
Return key, 17, 30, 55, 87–88
Right-edge marker, 110, 116
Right indent marker, 30, 32
Right justified text. *See* Justification
Right tab alignment, 33, 42
Rows, 50, 78–80
Ruler Line, 17, 27, 29–30, 37, 48

S

Save As command, 6–7, 14, 19, 58, 60, 69, 90–91, 95, 123
Save command, 6, 8, 14, 58, 60, 69, 90–91, 95
Saving
- database file, 90–91, 95
- file, 6–8
- spreadsheet, 58, 68–69
- word processing, 19

Scroll Bar, 2, 18, 52, 88, 91
Scroll box, 100–102
Scroll up, 18
Search menu
- Find, 43–44, 48
- Replace, 45–48

Select
  All command, 74, 80, 125
  button, 100–103, 115
  cell, 59
  defined, 3
  multiple rule, 101–102
  record, 92–93, 99–102
  Report, 114, 117
  text, 20, 24
Selected fields report, 115–117
Selection rules, 99–102, 115
Select menu, Find Cell, 52, 59
Self-test, 14–15, 25, 38, 48–49, 60, 71, 81–82, 95–96, 108, 120, 131
Set Cell Attributes command, 72–75, 80–81
Set Field Attributes, database, 85–86, 95
Shift key, 18, 53
Shift-return keystroke, 55
Shift-tab keystroke, 55
Show
  All Records, 100
  Clipboard command, 40, 75–76, 106
  Field Data command, 129
  Field Names command, 129–130
  Form command, 92–94, 104–105
  Formulas command, 77
  List command, 91, 93–94
  Ruler command, 29, 37
  Values command, 77
Shut Down command, 13
Size, character, 36, 116
Soft page breaks, 46
Sort
  command, 79–81, 98–99, 117
  dialog box, 79–80
  records, 98–99, 107
  rows, 78–81
Spacing, line, 36–37
Special menu, 13
Spelling, 22–23, 25
Spell menu, template, 65–66
Spreadsheet (SS)
  absolute reference, 63
  active cell, 51–52, 55
  cancel box, 54
  cell attributes, 72–75, 80–81
  change display format, 72–75
  column width, 63–67, 70
  copy and paste, 75–76
  copy cell contents, 62, 70
  correct errors, 55, 59
  create file, 50–51
  cut, 75–76
  data, 53–54
  delete columns, 76
  dollar sign, 63
  enter box, 54
  entry bar, 51, 54
  Fill Right command, 62, 70
  find cell, 53–54
  formulas, 56–59, 62–63, 77
  function, 67
  general format of, 74
  Insert command, 61–62
  justify text entry, 73–74
  label, 53
  move data, 78, 81
  move data to database, 123–125
  move data to word processor, 121–123
  numbers, 55–56, 59, 74–75
  number sign (#), 65
  print, 58–59, 69–70
  quotation mark, 53
  relative reference, 63
  save, 58, 68–69
  Show Formulas, 77
  Show Values, 77
  size, 52
  sort rows, 78–80
  Sum function, 67–68
  text, 53–55, 59
  Title Bar, 6
SS. *See* Spreadsheet
Start
  word processing, 16–19
  Works, 3
Style, spreadsheet, 73
Style command, 35–36
Sum function, spreadsheet, 67–68
Sum This Field command, 117
Switch between files, 9–10

T

Tab key, 55, 87–88, 111
Tabs, setting, 17, 32–33, 42–43, 48
Template, spreadsheet, 65–66
Temporary memory, 6
Text box, 7

Text entry
 spreadsheet, 53, 59, 73–74
 word processing, 17–18
Text field, database, 85
Text width, 37
Title, change report, 110
Title Bar, defined, 2
Toggle switches, 73
TotalPage menu, 117, 120

U

Underline, 35–36, 73
Untitled, 6
Update record, 94
Uppercase letters, 18, 53

V

Values, constant, 53, 77
Vertical scroll bar, 92

W

Window, 2
Window menu
 desktop files, 9–10, 78
 Help, 12–14
 Hide Clipboard, 40
 Show Clipboard, 40, 75–76, 106
Word processing (WP)
 blank lines, 18
 bold, 35–36
 center text, 34–35
 character size, 36
 check spelling, 22–23
 copy format, 37
 copy text, 21, 24
 correct errors, 18
 create document, 16–17
 delete text, 18–20, 24
 enter text, 17–18
 font, 36
 footers, 47
 format document, 27
 headers, 47
 icon, 16
 insert text, 21–22, 24
 justification, 34–35, 40–42, 48
 line indentation, 29–30
 line spacing, 36–37
 margin settings, 28–29
 move data to word processor, 121–123
 move text, 20–21, 24
 page breaks, 46–48
 page numbering, 47
 paragraph indentation, 16–17, 31–32
 print text, 23–25
 replace text, 21–22, 24, 48
 retrieve file, 10–11, 26
 Ruler Line, 17, 27, 29–30, 37, 48
 save file, 19
 search for text, 48
 select text, 20, 24
 spelling checking, 22–23
 start, 16
 tabs, 17, 32–33, 42–43, 48
 Title Bar, 6
 underline, 35–36
 word wrap, 18
Word wrap, 18
Works icon, 3
Works Startup disk, 4
WP. *See* Word processing